Conditions of a Solitary Bird

A Total Critical Analysis
Of the Works of
Carlos Castaneda

By

Gordon Richiusa

&

LIVING THE WARRIOR'S LIFE
by
Kumu Michelle Manu

Gordon Richiusa

Conditions of a Solitary Bird

Copyright 2024 Gordon Richiusa

ISBN: 978-0-9829926-6-1

All rights reserved. Printed on acid-free paper. No part of this publication may be reproduced, stored in a retrieval system, or transmitted in any form or by any means, electronic, mechanical, recording or otherwise, without the prior written permission of the author.

Published in the United States by Five Birds Publications, For Heroes' Hearts® Inc.
2490 EastShore Place Unit K110, Reno NV 89509

This book is not intended as libelous, slanderous or to caste a negative pall on any person either living or dead. The contents are completely the views of the author. Any opinions or statements made by the author are intended for clarification and educational purposes.

Edited by Thomas Hardie
Cover Design: Jesse Horsting

Gordon Richiusa

Conditions of a Solitary Bird

Acknowledgments

I would like to give my thanks to all those who have helped me with the completion of of both my thesis and the current work. My Thesis Advisors included Professors Reid, Marcus and Newman; Proofreading was done by Joanne Sparber and Charlene Bones originally. A special thank you to Professor John Stafford, without whose help and encouragement I probably would not have graduated and this current work would have never been started, let alone completed. In addition, this compilation-edition has been greatly improved by direct and indirect assistance from Jhoon Rhee, Jesse Horsting, Dana Stamos, Maria Arvelo, Barbara Rich, Brian Wallace, John Harrison, Ernie Peters (Longwalker), Michelle Manu, Renee Baribeau, and Amy Wallace (among others who may not have wished to be named).

Conditions of a Solitary Bird

Table of Contents

PART ONE
PREFACE ...p. 11
Original ABSTRACT ...p. 23
1. INTRODUCTION ...p. 25
2. THE ROLE(S) ...p. 33
3. FOUR BOOKS, ONE STORY ...p. 55
4. TRACING PERSONAL HISTORY. ...p. 87
5. FROM PLATO TO JUANCHO ...p.119
6. ANTHROPOLOGY OR ART? ...p.137
7. CONCLUSION ...p.153
APPENDIX ...p.159
BIBLIOGRAPHY for Part One. ...p.163

PART TWO
RESTART ...p. 167
Literary Lessons & Capsules ...p.171
8. THE SECOND RING OF POWER ...p.175
9. THE EAGLE'S GIFT. ...p.177
10. THE FIRE FROM WITHIN ...p.178
11. THE POWER OF SILENCE ...p.179
12. THE ART OF DREAMING ...p.179
13. MAGICAL PASSES ...p.182
14. THE WHEEL OF TIME ...p.183
15. THE ACTIVE SIDE OF INFINITY ...p.184
16. RECONCILIATION AND DSS ...p.187
17. LIVING A WARRIOR'S LIFE ...p.225

Gordon Richiusa

PREFACE

Before reading any further, or giving it any thought try to answer this question: *Are you a Dragon or a Dragon Slayer?*

As a lover of words who has made a healthy living with my hobby (teacher/curriculum developer, editor, publisher/producer writer, and journalist) I have learned a few things about the power of words, and shared many thoughts on the subject. While words are just human sounds in special patterns we recognize that allow humans to communicate with one another about our ideas, beliefs, and feelings, ALL creatures to some degree communicate at these levels.

I've learned to rely on my words and respect them to the point that I sometimes take my time before expressing my feelings, because our ability to communicate also helps us focus on defining our own beliefs. They make us feel superior to all other creatures because, we believe (wrongly) that this ability to cast spells over ourselves and others with sounds is the thing that sets us above all other species. It has taken me over 50 years to finish this book for publication, for this reason.

Societies—even empires—are created and destroyed based upon nothing but a shared belief, which often draws strength from nothing more than clever words. Oftentimes, our myths--originally intended to aid us in giving human shape to the unfathomable--claim to detail how not only the Earth, but Reality came into existence, helping us to greatly exaggerate the importance of the human species and especially our self-love of words, *"In the beginning was the word, and the word was God."*

Often, those word-smiths we admire use imagery in the form of comparisons and contrasts to make our beliefs even more clear to ourselves as well as to convince others of the specialness of our words. Rebus writing is picture writing, considered a primitive form of communication, because it does not rely on words to communicate.

The most common technique for this double edged sword is empathy...the ability to see oneself as having a similar perspective as others, or to convince the other person that they are somehow, *just like you. We observe the world from our narrow perspective and then try to either claim powers not generally associated with humans, or fill in the blanks of our snap judgements with magical thinking. Extended imagery and techniques such as personification (creating a character that represents things we call bigger than life) help us express complicated, or perhaps unpopular ideas hold a special attraction for humans.*

Carlos hit on some universal imagery (either by accident or design) in his scenery and characterizations of Don Juan Mateus, Don Genaro, Carlos, La Gorda, and all the rest. This is why I call his books *literature*. It's why I completed my Master of Arts in English Literature by analyzing

Castaneda's books. In addition, I have used the words of Carlos Castaneda to great and broad benefit throughout my life. As a teacher of martial arts I saw a template for the student-teacher relationship (that was not associated with any religious practice such as Zen) which focused on self awareness and personal responsibility that favored empathy, teaching by example, and a student-focused approach. Every student is broadly different, yet all are trying to understand the same narrow/specific things.

Although I can procrastinate with the best of them, I have used this crossover between ideas, to my own immediate benefit, taking some of Don Juan's and Carlos's lessons and adjusting them.

In **Tales of Power** the character Carlos (literally both a sorcerer's apprentice and academic) reads to the character of Don Juan a poem entitled, <u>The Conditions of a Solitary Bird.</u>

The imagery of this poem transcends multiple disciplines. I read it in the Castaneda books, but it was also recited to me by some of my martial arts instructors.

Here are some of my own unique (some say odd) perspectives which have been distilled from years of coping by using thoughts, word meanings, and actions in combination. This is one of the great lessons I've learned through my association with the works of Carlos Castaneda. Human beings have the remarkable capacity to create useful new patterns while seamlessly selecting and analyzing the old. The character Don Juan summarized these three levels of attention or awareness as the first, second, and third attention. This spot is coincidentally at the crossroads of the Known, The Unknown, and the Unknowable.

So here I say that there are just two main types of people. I've always been told that one of my strengths is distilling complicated ideas into simple, understandable forms. For the sake of making this complicated idea as simple as possible I call these two archetypes: *Dragons* and Dragon-*Slayers*.

Now let's return to the first sentences of this book's PREFACE: *Are You A Dragon or a Dragon Slayer?* Everyone was forced to answer this question in different ways, based on preconceptions or even without knowing any details. That's one of the little tricks I teach my writing students: Start Your Writing with a Question? It is in our human nature to try and answer every question and this helps to motivate the reader to look ahead.

You may have forgotten about this question until now, but I hope you already answered or perhaps argued with my premise. It really doesn't matter which one (Dragon or Dragon Slayer) that you identify with (if either) or how you define these terms--most people are going to be able to pick their type right away and be able to not only accept the premise of this thesis, but understand and accept that this human tendency seems to be a major factor in how we relate to the one another and make all our decisions. It causes us to say yes or *no* to every new idea, until we're directed that the idea was actually an old one to begin with--something that is *common sense*, or that *people have known for a long time.*

In other words it is **in our human nature** to be in this constant state of anxiety, one thing always seen as good and right and the other not...but which is which? In the heat of the survival moment it generally doesn't matter what we decide. There is an axiom which states, "that which doesn't kill us makes us stronger." However, the truth is that a decision which didn't kill us just didn't kill us, yet. Indeed, every time we make a choice we have a tendency to commit fully to it. This comes from many generations of human species being forced by sudden circumstance to make split-second decisions. Ideas like, Fight or Flight are wrongly accepted as our only two choices. We've heard it said, "Life is full of choices." Unfortunately, we often don't have enough information, or time to make the perfect choice in an emergency that we are going to be comfortable with in the future, but not choosing is usually the worst thing we can do. In self defense when harm is imminent we say, "anything is better than nothing."

Truly healthy and happy people use the tried and true Trial And Error Method for problem solving, admitting that new information might change their thought process as well as their decisions. On the other hand, each of us may also find we are happy in the middle ground of **good enough.**

When it comes to personal perception, there is plenty of self-delusion to go around. I'm not pointing any fingers which I have not already pointed squarely at myself. None of us can cast the first delusion. Yet, most of us do act and eventually come around to on similar solutions to every question…not because what we land on is the best solution, but because we're all just trying to sort things out in our own heads with the least pain. Additionally, if we have an ounce of empathy, we accept our differences in the same light as our

Conditions of a Solitary Bird

similarities as well as be willing to accept that some might be using our basic human instincts against us. You know the old saying, "You can fool some of the people all of the time." After all, we are all humans.

When we start to accept that humans have this Dragon Slayer tendency this might give way to two other potential problems. One deals with Mob Mentality...not only why brainwashing works but also why some brains seem to *need* washing. The catch in all this--and this is the key point I want to make-- is that, or course **there are *no such things as dragons.***

Gordon Richiusa

Conditions of a Solitary Bird

The following was submitted in partial
satisfaction of the
requirements for the degree of
Master of Arts
in
Department of English
to
CALIFORNIA STATE UNIVERSITY,
NORTHRIDGE
entitled
THE CONDITIONS OF A SOLITARY BIRD
**(AN ANALYSIS OF THE WORKS OF
CARLOS CASTANEDA)**

by
Gordon Frank Richiusa

Gordon Richiusa

PART ONE

ABSTRACT
To Original Thesis

The following is a "total critical" examination of four of the works of Carlos Castaneda; The Teachings of Don Juan, A Separate Reality, Journey to Ixtlan, and Tales of Power. This mode of analysis is based on Professor Robert Reid III's Ph.D. dissertation contention that works of literature, instead of being analyzed from a single perspective should be examined from several perspectives to insure a more encompassing evaluation of a work's literary merits.

I have taken Professor Reid's thesis and used it as a starting point for this study, and have, therefore, divided this paper into chapter sections with each section dealing with a separate aspect of the Castaneda works. Within this framework I have strived to interrelate the individual sections not only to one another but each section to three overriding assumptions that I have made about the works in question. The first assumption is that the Castaneda books are literature (whether they are factual accounts, as the author contends or fictional works as many believe). The second assumption is that these books are worthy of study from all the perspectives, including the total critical perspective. And third, I have assumed that the four books, although enjoyable as units each unto themselves, should be read together as a total unit to grasp these works' full impact.

This study has led me to the conclusions that these three assumptions are facts and the importance of this study therefore is derived as much from the process itself (the total critical analytic process) as from the results of inquiry.

Conditions of a Solitary Bird

1. THESIS INTRODUCTION

Since 1968 when the first book of the Castaneda series appeared on the sellers shelves, literally millions have been kept spellbound by the wit, magic, struggles and, in short, the various <u>doings</u> and <u>not-doings</u> of two brilliantly drawn characters, an old Yaqui Indian sorcerer called Don Juan Matus and his innocuous apprentice, a student from U.C.L.A., named Carlos Castaneda.

What has been most fascinating as we trudged up and down hills and across deserts, learned from and were baffled by the various teachings of Don Juan, is the diversity of responses and reactions that the four books, <u>The Teachings of Don Juan</u>, <u>A Separate Reality</u>, <u>Journey to Ixtlan</u>, and <u>Tales of Power</u> have generated. While the books have been bitterly attacked as much as praised, even the most violent detractors all seem to find something, in some way positive to say about the books.

The key point of objection seems to stem from either an intrinsic dislike of the ideas that were being expounded or a disbelief in the major controversial contention of Castaneda's that the books were completely factual accounts.

It was not until recently that the question of their value on a purely artistic level has been even considered. Unfortunately, the phrase "literary value" always seems, in these cases, to take on a pejorative sense. Very few people are willing to accept the fact that popular, possibly non-fictional, works were actually well written, which could indeed account for much of their popularity. This has recently changed somewhat as is evidenced by the remarkable fact that I, a Master's candidate, was allowed to write my thesis on these books.

Anthropologists were analyzing from their own information-gathering perspective. Drug aficionados (anthropologists in their own right) scrutinized new ways to absorb intoxicating chemicals. Philosophers followed the philosophy of

Conditions of a Solitary Bird

the books and compared them to Plato, Blake, Wittgenstein and others. Eastern cultists were forever finding similarities between the teachings of Juan and Suzuki's book of Zen. All those who examined these books from their own perspectives found good and bad qualities in each text. But one perspective was overlooked and that we shall name what Dr. Robert Reid III named it in his doctoral dissertation, the "total critical perspective."[1]

I was introduced to the term in 1972, but it was not until recently, when struck by some words of Don Juan's in a passage from Tales of Power that the concept took me in its own totality.

Only if one pits two views against each other can one weasel between them to arrive at the real world... I meant; that one can arrive at the totality of oneself only when one fully understands that the

---

[1] Robert Franklin Reid, III Process and Criticism: A Theory of Meaning (University of Pittsburgh, 1973)

world is merely a view, regardless of whether that view belongs to an ordinary man or a sorcerer.[2]

The total critical perspective points out that obviously there are a number of views from which one may judge and analyze a work of literature. Seldom, if ever, are all views considered of equal value. The total critical perspective labels these more general perspectives using terms set down by Myer Abrams in <u>The Mirror and the Lamp</u>. These general perspectives are 'mimetic,' 'expressive,' and 'pragmatic.' These are divided into more specialized areas, such as scholarship, content, form, textuality, and texture. It is not my intention to flippantly restate in brief what Professor Reid so painstakingly prepared after years of research and diligent labor.[3] Let it suffice to say that the method, which was named above will be the one used in this thesis. It is for this reason that the thesis has been broken up

---

[2] Carlos Castaneda, <u>Tales of Power</u> (new York: Simon and Schuster, 1974), p. 240

[3] Contact Professor Reid at C.S.U.N. for further information.

into chapter sections so that we might examine the parts separately with comments made intermittently as to how the parts relate to the whole. Thus, we hope to adhere to a more total critical perspective, than any that have been applied to the Castaneda series thus far.

This choice was made not only in a kind of aesthetic response to the basic proposition of the four Castaneda books about the nature of reality, but also, because of the diversity of subjects and areas of interest that the four books touch upon. And because of the relationship that the author has created with his characters I felt that biographical material about the author would be a good starting point for this examination.

The second chapter "The Role of Carlos, Carlitos, and Castaneda the Author," follows the development of the character of "Carlos" in the text as well as "Castaneda" of the authorial world, but also investigates some possible explanations for these developments and the symbiotic relationship that the character "Carlos" and the author "Castaneda" established throughout the thirteen year period during which the books were written.

The third chapter, "Four Books, One Story," deals mainly with the style of presentation, where evidence will be submitted to justify my contention that although each book was presented as an individual entity, the four books can and, indeed should be examined as a single unit.

The fourth chapter is of a highly fact-searching nature and is called "Tracing Personal History; Character Development of the Main Character." Here I deal almost exclusively with what we know about the characters of the books from the books themselves. The main emphasis of course is on Don Juan and Genaro. But all characters will find a spot in this discussion.

In the fifth chapter, "Prom Plato to Juancho," I attempt to root out possible strains of influence in the philosophy of the books.

Conditions of a Solitary Bird

In the sixth chapter, I get to the source of the major problem of accepting the four books as factual accounts. This chapter is entitled "Anthropology or Art" and in it I discuss also possibly the greatest barrier for acceptance that these works have encountered, the problem of translation. The conclusion, of course, brings all these considerations to a close and sorts out what has been achieved by this study.

Gordon Richiusa

2. THE ROLES OF CARLOS, CARLITOS, AND CASTANEDA THE AUTHOR

Among those relationships that exist between the author and his characters, there perhaps can be found no parallel for that which has been created between Carlos Castaneda and the character "Carlos." There are a number of very interesting peculiarities involved in this relationship. In this chapter we will discuss solely the character of Carlos, However, this discussion of a single character will necessitate a kind of splintering in a schizophrenic sense of the word. For during the course of the four books not only did the books themselves develop a fascinating, even classic character for the reader, but also the author Carlos Castaneda developed into a character of fascination himself. There was a 'synchronized' development.

Before we survey the intricate character of Carlos, his function and purpose, let us discuss Castaneda the man. Then we might be better able to get a grasp on the ***psychosynchrosymbiosis***, the mutual need, that the two Carlos' developed for one another. This need emerged from a single mind, yet produced two separate, complex personalities that began to rely on each other for their very existence, as well as their development.

To understand the various possible reasons for the creation of all this psychosynchrosymbiosis one must first be convinced of the existence of more than one character, a *Carlos* of the books as separate from the Carlos of the authorial world. Therefore, I will first trace a bit of each character's personal history.

What do we know about Carlos the character solely from what is written in the texts about him? His biographical sketch would go something like this: Carlos attended college at the University of California at Los Angeles during the summer of 1960 and, we must assume, during some semesters previous and following. Somewhere in the course of this same summer, Carlos met an old Yaqui Indian in a bus depot in an Arizona border town. The *teachings* that would culminate in his gaining membership in the world of sorcery, began on June 23, 1961. Carlos had read **The Tibetan Book of the Dead**[4], some poems by Juan Ramon Jiminez entitled, *El Viage Definitivio (The Definitive Journey)*[5], a poem by Juan de la Cruz from ***Dichos de Luz y Amor***[6] and (we are again forced to assume) at least a few books on botany and anthropology (his major). Before he became an apprentice, when Carlos was six years old, we are told that his mother abandoned him. When he was eight, he spent the most hellish year of his life circulating among his mother's sisters. On this experience Carlos goes on to say:

"Each of my aunts had a large family, and no matter how careful and protective the aunts were

---

[4] According to Carlos Castenada in *A Separate Reality;Further Conversations with Don Juan (New York; Simon and Schuster, 1971, p.193)*

[5] Carlos Castenada, **Journey to Ixtlan; The Lessons of Don Juan** (New York; Simon and Schuster, 1972) p. 266

[6] Castaneda, Tales of Power, Epigraph.

toward me, I had twenty-two cousins to contend with. Their cruelty was sometimes bizarre. I felt then that I was surrounded by enemies, and in the excruciating years that followed I waged a desperate and sordid war...which logically extended to the school grounds."[7]

Carlos continues this personal anecdote about his ruthless school years. He attended rural schools where the first and third graders were "separated only by a space between desks." Then, he met a little flat-nosed first grader who had been nicknamed "Button-nose." Carlos used to pick on this boy (who name was actually Joaquin) haphazardly, but little Joaquin still seemed to like Carlos in spite of everything he did to him. One day, Carlos deliberately toppled over a large standing blackboard;

"It fell on him (Joaquin); the desk in which he was sitting absorbed some of the impact, but still the blow broke his collar bone." Carlos was greatly affected by this incident and vowed to never be victorious again, if Joaquin could be cured. This, we

---

[7] Ibid, p. 117.

are told was the main reason Carlos could not change as easily as Don Juan would have liked."[8]

Another interesting tale we are told about the early events of Carlos' life, revolves around his years on his grandfather's leghorn chicken farm, where he hunted a large number of birds:

"It all began with my grandfather's explosion of anger upon taking count of his young chickens. They had been disappearing in a steady and disconcerting manner."

The historical Carlos continue this story of how the caue of the disappearance was discovered to be a white falcon, that Carlos was goaded by his grandfather to hunt. The recollection of this event is ended when Carlos, having the bird in his rifle sight, decides not to shoot.[9]

When Carlos was older, he had a beautiful blonde girlfriend, whom he lost because he was *accessible,* as Don Juan puts it; "You were always

---

[8] Castaneda, A Separate Reality, pp.140-141

[9] Castaneda, Journey to Ixtlan, p. 31

within her reach and your life was a routine one." This, of course was another barrier that Carlos needed to overcome to be able to benefit from the sorcery teachings.[10]

In <u>Journey to Ixtlan</u> Carlos tells us that he'd always wanted to be an artist but was not successful. "I always wanted to be an artist and for years I'd tried my hand at that. I still have the painful memory of my failure."[11] Carlos seems to have a lot of painful memories, which we are told about in a nebulous fashion on a number of occasions, and they stem usually from his dislike of himself. Another representative passage in <u>Journey to Ixtlan</u> begins as most of the others do, when something indescribable aroused some deeply buried emotions in Carlos.

I began to talk about my life. I confessed that I had never respected or liked anybody, not even myself, and that I had always felt that I was inherently evil, and thus my attitude towards others

---

[10] Ibid.,p.69

[11] Ibid., p. 81

was always veiled with a certain bravado and daring.[12]

During the course of the entire series of novels, there are only a few passages that deal with the personal history of the character Carlos, and not once, anywhere in the four books is there even a hint of a description of his physical appearance. But then, the books are supposed to be of a nonfiction nature, and one is to assume that the *character* of Carlos looks like, and in fact IS the author Castaneda. This just simply is not the case, that is, as far as the new facts will bear out. What is meant by this is that we really don't know which facts to believe or which to disbelieve, or how far to associate the character Carlos with the author Caataneda. Nor, do we know if what we are told about the *man* Castaneda is any less a creation, in a literary sense, than what we are told about the character *Carlos.* There may very well be an authorial *Carlitos* who is purposefully fictionalizing

---

[12] Ibid., p. 183

what we know about the character in the books; there may also be an author who is taking a bit of poetic license with what he is choosing to share with us about Castaneda. Thus, the schizophrenic gap continues to grow into, perhaps self-created, but insurmountable chasm.

In February of 1973 an interview with Carlos Casteneda appeared in Harper's Magazine. A totally trusting interviewer very wisely allowed the, by then *Doctor* Castaneda (Ph.D) to speak freely and without interruption about his past and future. The story in this article sounds remarkably like that which one might piece together by sorting out information from the Castaneda books.

"I was born in Brazil. My mother died when I was little, so I was reared on my grandfather's farm by eight aunts. My father was a professor—he was usually away teaching. When I was fifteen, I came to Los Angeles to live with a family here and go to Hollywood High. I went to UCLA and tried art and psychology before I decided on anthropology."[13]

---

[13] Gwyneth Cravens, *Talking to Power and Spinning with the Ally,* Harpers Magazine, February 1973, p. 03

Conditions of a Solitary Bird

At first glance there seems to be little or no difference between the character of Carlos and his authorial counterpart. The only new information deals with the period of Carlos' life for which we have no facts in the books, that period from early teens to the writing of the doctoral dissertation in anthropology. Unfortunately, when more *facts* are compiled—when Castaneda is allowed to speak freely and uninterruptedly about his personal history—some very interesting implausibilities emerge.

In a more exhaustive and enterprising article than the one in *Harper's*, a *Time Magazine* team took the trouble not only to let Castaneda speak freely, but also to check what he said against verifiable records. The result is surprising at first reading, but then upon reflection less so.

In a biographical segment in the *Times* article, Castaneda's account of his life and the researcher's are pitted against one another. Following is perhaps the most complete, printed account of how Castaneda described the events of his life from birth to *The Don Juan Days*. This section is important enough to be quoted here, at length:

"By his own account, Castaneda was not his original name. He was born he said, to a well-known but anonymous family in Sao Paulo, Brazil, on Christmas day, 1935. His father, who later became a professor of literature, was then seventeen and his mother fifteen. Because his parents were so immature, little Carlos was packed off to be raised by his maternal grandparents on a chicken farm in the back country of Brazil...When Carlos was six, his story runs, his parents took him back and lavished guilty affection on him...a year later, his mother died...Now Carlos was left with his father... Castaneda describes his father's efforts to become a writer as a farce of indecision, but he adds, "I am my father."...Carlos was put into a very proper Buenos Aires boarding school, Nicolas Avellaneda. He says he stayed there until he was fifteen, acquiring the Spanish (he already spoke Italian and Portuguese) in which he would later interview Don Juan. But, he became so unmanageable that an uncle, the family patriarch had him placed with a foster family in Los Angeles. In 1951 Carlos moved to the U.S. and enrolled at Hollywood High. Graduating two years later, he tried a course in sculpture at Milan's Academy of Fine Arts, but, "I did not have the sensitivity or the openness to be a great artist." Depressed, in crisis, he headed back to Los Angeles and started a course in social

psychology at U.C.L.A. shifting later to an anthropology course. Says he, "I really threw my life out the window. I said to myself, if it's going to work, it must be new." In 1959 he formally changed his name to Castaneda."[14]

What follows next is also to be found in this same exhaustive article and is what was discovered about Carlos Castaneda, the author, from public records and apart from any intermediation on Castaneda's part.

"Between 1955 and 1959 Carlos Castaneda was enrolled, under that name, as a pre-psychology major at Los Angeles City College. His liberal studies included, in his first two years, two courses in creative writing and one in journalism. Vernon King, his creative writing professor at L.A.C.C. still has a copy of **The Teachings of Don Juan,** *inscribed "To a great teacher, Vernon King, from one of his students, Carlos Castaneda." Moreover, immigration records show that a Carlos Cesar Arana Castaneda did indeed enter the U.S. at San Francisco when the author said he did, in 1951. This Castaneda too was 5 ft. 5 in., weighed 140 pounds and came from Latin America. But, he was Peruvian, born on Christmas Day, 1925, in the*

---

[14] *Don Juan and the Sorcerer's Apprentice,* TIME, March 5, 1973, p.43.

ancient Inca town of Cajamarca, which makes him 48, not 38 this year...His father was NOT an academic, but a goldsmith and watchmaker named Cesar Arana Burungaray. His mother, Susana Castaneda Navoa, died not when Carlos was six but when he was twenty-four. Her son spent three years in the local high school in Cajamarca and then moved with his family to Lima in 1948, when he graduated from the Colegio Natienal de Nuestra Senora de Guadalupe and then studied painting and sculpture, NOT in Milan, but at the National Fine Arts School of Peru. One of his fellow students there, Jose Bracamonte remembers his pal Carlos as a resourceful blade who lived mainly off gambling (cards, horses, and dice) and harbored "like an obsession" the wish to move to the U.S. "We all liked Carlos," recalls Bracamonte. "He was witty, imaginative, cheerful—a big liar, and a real friend." ...Castaneda apparently wrote home sporadically, at least until 1969, the year after "Don Juan" came out. His cousin, Lucy Chavez, who was raised with him "like a sister," still keeps his letters. They indicate that he served in the U.S. Army, and left it after suffering a slight wound or "nervous shock"—Lucy is not sure which. (The Defense Department, however, has no record of Carlos Castaneda's service.)"*[15]*

---

[15] Ibid., p. 44.

Conditions of a Solitary Bird

In arriving at the importance of all this, the overwhelming consensus among those who wrote about Carlos Castaneda seems to set up a major problem: Are Castaneda's books as big a fabrication as the story of his life which he told to a number of reporters and interviewers?

It is obvious that Carlos is just as big a liar as Jose Bracamonte says that he is. Where I differ with past researchers is in the relative importance of the lies and the importance of the fact that lies were told at all.

The basic thesis of Richard DeMille's book, ***Castaneda's Journey: The Power and the Allegory*** is that if Castaneda told these lies, it follows that he is lying about his books being non-fiction. Many other researchers, on the other hand, dismiss Castaneda's personal creativity by saying that Carlos has a right to absolute control over his identity and besides, he is a sorcerer and not to be bothered with his past.[16]

There are strengths to both of these perspectives. However, could we not take both arguments one step further and ask still another question about the significance of the *untruths?* If indeed the author Carlos Castaneda has falsified information about the events of his life, should we not assume that those facts he has chosen to alter or create in whole were selected with the same deliberation and purposefulness that any author would be assumed to possess?

Then, one wonders if ANY of the so-called *verifiable facts* are valid as well. It is totally possible, taking the scope of these likely fabrications that nothing that we know about the man Castaneda is valid. Might not one who willingly lies to his own cousin about service in the U.S. armed forces be likely to falsify an easy few

---

[16] Richard DeMille, ***Castaneda's Journey: The Power and the Allegory*** (Santa Barbara: Capa Press, 1976).

numerals on the date of his birth certificate? Looked at in this light, could we not then ask why Castaneda *chose* to be born on Christmas Day? Is there room for a discussion of a possible messianic complex? Richard DeMille questioned a number of people on how they felt about the possibility that the Don Juan of the books was a fictional character. One response deserves quoting on this point: "Don Juan is the most important model for a man since Jesus. If he is imaginary, then Carlos Castaneda is the principle psychological, spiritual and literary genius of recent generations."[17] Complements like this could go to ones head were one not possessed of the humility of a sorcerer, such as Castaneda is professed to be.

On another count, if the author's father was an academic, the symbol for a young academic struggling to break the bonds of his past begins to stretch over generations and becomes allegory. However, if we are to assume the *verifiable facts*

---

[17] Ibid., p. 24.

are correct, and that the author's father was a goldsmith and watchmaker, an equally all-encompassing symbol dealing with a value system that transcends any one social or monetary begins to take shape, or one that relates to the Don Juanian view that all experience is recollection and that *time* has no meaning.

Going to the Castaneda texts for a moment, we might try to flesh out at least one of those symbols briefly. In ***Separate Reality***, for instance Carlos tells Don Juan of a deep feeling of despondency and hopelessness, which he experienced at the sight of a group of youngsters eating leftovers from a table at a restaurant. "I left that city feeling that there was no hope for those children whose world was already molded by their day after day struggle for crumbs."

Don Juan uses this sympathy in Carlos, as always, to make Carlos feel ridiculous and also to make a point:

"Didn't you once tell me that in your opinion man's greatest accomplishment was to become a man of knowledge? ...Then, how could you feel sorry for those children? Any one of them could

become a man of knowledge. All the men of knowledge I know were kids like those you saw eating leftovers and licking the tables."[18]

Can this not be seen to relate to a subtle sub-theming (at least in this one book) dealing with values, in general? Incredibly, this theme actually does continue as important throughout the entire series. In ***Journey to Ixtlan***, Don Juan calls Carlos a *pimp* for his anthropological work, implying Carlos was not working for his own pleasure but merely pimping for the university. In ***Tales of Power***, when Don Juan has Carlos examining for comparison people in a park in Mexico City, some of the most pathetic passersby are obviously well-off financially.

The question is then, could one *reverse* the direction of this plot-theme, traveling *from* the fourth book of the series, through the first and all the way back to the source of the works, *the author*, to continue to look for clues to symbols of

---

[18] Castaneda, ***A Separate Reality***, p. 22.

perspective and belief? Has Carlos Castaneda, the author, become so integrated into his works *by intention and design* that we must disbelieve or, at least, closely scrutinize any and all information that he reveals to us? The answer, I feel is *yes*.

What we will never know however, is whether or not the books are totally fictions or possibly only partially based on fact. Carlos Castaneda is a sorcerer, whether or not he made up the ground rules and outlined the requirements himself. He is now required by his own invention to comply with the dictums of the system. He has gained membership in the world of sorcerers and his personal history is indeed his own.

It is not since Conan Doyle perhaps, that an author has been so closely associated with his character. The difference is that there is no reluctance on the author's part, in this case, to disassociate himself from his invention. "Carlos" needs Castaneda, but Castaneda needs "Carlos" as well. Therefore a combined personality emerges, a

Conditions of a Solitary Bird

"Carlitos," a trickster that classically instructs as he fools his students, that lies yet speaks with a honeyed tongue, a teacher or 'benefactor' that has knowledge and secrets to share if only truth can be discerned from falsehood. It is not remarkable then that when "Carlos," in Journey to Ixtlan gains membership in the sorcerer's world and acquires a spirit helper in animal form[19] that the animal is a coyote, a creature in literature from many cultures as well as a series of Yaqui Myths that is known as "Trickster." 'The only sad part," Don Juan tells Carlos after the latter narrates the 'extraordinary experience' of talking to a coyote on a hilltop and having the coyote talk back ". . . is that coyotes are not reliable. They are tricksters. It is your fate not to have a dependable animal companion .... If I were you, I would never trust a Coyote. But [he adds

---

[19] Castaneda, A Separate Reality, p. 38. Definition of ally (spirit helper): "they are forces, neither good or bad, just forces that a brujo learns to harness."

significantly] you are different and you may even become a coyote sorcerer."[20]

Indeed it looks as though 'Carlos' has become a coyote sorcerer and Castaneda a coyote writer. He has set himself apart from his loved ones and has bewitched many a reader into a kind of demonic allegiance to his cause.[21]

As an epigraph to the fourth book of the series, Castaneda quotes from "Dichos de Luz y Amor," by San Juan de la Cruz, a sixteenth century Spanish priest. This poem lists the "Conditions of a Solitary Bird," an actual species, but the verse takes on spiritual connotations for Juan.

Besides learning about this poem in the Castaneda Books, I was recite this poem by Zen and Western Archery teachers, martial arts masters, and Indigenous Elders in both academic and esoteric courses of investigation to describe how we

---

[20] Castaneda, Journey to Ixtlan, p. 254.

[21] DeMille, p. 13. Al Egori claims to possess a photograph of Don Juan but refuses to expose it to anyone.

Conditions of a Solitary Bird

problem solve and establish how and when we've achieved success. I even used it to describe a beautifully constructed poem, essay, or story. It was written by a 15th Century Franciscan Catholic Monk in Mexico named San Juan De La Cruz (describing we must assume, what it means to be a good Catholic).

> *The conditions of a solitary bird are five.*
> *The first is that it flies to the highest point;*
> *The second that it aims its beak to the skies;*
> *The third, is that it does not suffer for want of company, not even of its own kind;*
> *The fourth, that it has no definite color;*
> *And, the fifth is that it sings very softly.*
> —San Juan De La Cruz

Carlos Castaneda has fulfilled these difficult conditions. He has made it so, and now, even if Castaneda himself produced four more books proving that Don Juan could not possibly exist it really wouldn't matter. How could we believe him?

The achievement is supreme and would be noteworthy even if the books were not extraordinary apart from their relationship with the writer. It is indeed the literary world's great fortune that this is not the case.

3. FOUR BOOKS, ONE STORY
THE STYLE OF PRESENTATION

In this section, I will discuss the style of presentation that Carlos Castaneda chose for his tetralogy and elaborate the contention that although each book can be read as a single unit, they read best and are understood most if considered as a single unit "in total." The phrase "style of presentation" refers to the manner in which the author chooses to relate his story.

First, let us summarize the main action and thrust of the novels individually so that we might better understand their relationship and connection and more easily follow their conceptual flow.

The Teaching of Don Juan begins with a dedication by the author for "Don Juan and those two persons who shared his sense of magical time with me."[22] Next is a forward by Walter

---

[22] Carlos Castaneda, the Teachings of Don Juan: A Yaqui way of Knowledge (new York: Ballantine Books, 1969)

Goldschmidt, which begins, "This book is both ethnography and allegory." Following this is an *acknowledgements* page and finally an *introduction* by the author.

The introduction is rather lengthy (14 pages) and attempts to establish an academic tone and disguise for the narrator who is known simply as *Carlos*. We are told the details of Carlos' meeting with his informant Don Juan Matus and the establishment of the teacher-apprentice link between these two, which, it is revealed, lasted for four years (1961-1964) and was broken off voluntarily by the apprentice. The book idea was not conceived until several months later. Of significance also is the narrator's belief that the "acquisition of an ally, meant exclusively the exploitation of states of non-ordinary reality he (Don Juan) produced in me through the use of hallucinogenic plants."[23]

---

[23] Ibid, p 13

Conditions of a Solitary Bird

The main body of the book is divided into two sections. The first section is labeled "The Teachings" and is composed of eleven chapters which are, in turn, dated by day of the week, month date and year. There are a number of datings in each chapter which gives the first section the appearance and the reading pace of a journal. The first chapter introduces Don Juan and establishes the character of Carlos, the narrator, as a classic, cocky, naïve academic who doesn't know as much about the world as he thinks he does. Don Juan, of course, is the wise old Indian who takes it upon himself for some unknown reason to teach Carlos about his shortcomings and about the mystery and beauty of the world. This, we are to assume, is something an academic is not well versed in. The bulk of the work follows Carlos, a young U.C.L.A. anthropology student, as he learns the esoteric requirements of an apprentice sorcerer. The "Teachings" end after Carlos has been subjected to a nightmarish battle for his life against a female sorcerer and has decided he must cease the lessons in order to maintain his physical and mental safety. There is a brief afterword, which indicates in mildly definite terms that he (the narrator) has given up his quest for Don Juan's esoteric knowledge.

"That experience was the last of Don Juan's 3 teachings . . . ever since that time I have refrained from seeking his lessons. And, although Don Juan has not changed his benefactor's attitude toward me, I do believe that I have succumbed to the first enemy of a man of knowledge."[24]

The second section is entitled "A Structural Analysis." It is a summary in outline form of the ideas expressed in his teachings. "A structural scheme abstracted from the data on the states of non-ordinary reality presented in the foregoing parts of this book, conceived as an attempt to disclose the internal cohesion and the cogency of Don Juan's teachings."[25]

---

[24] Ibid, p 198

[25] Ibid, p 201

Conditions of a Solitary Bird

The tone is extremely academic, even more than the "Teachings" section. The great difference between the two (aside from one being mainly summary and the other narrative-descriptive in nature) is the feeling of detachment and objectivity the narrator's "voice" seems to take on.

After the second section are two appendices. Appendix A is called "The Process of Validating Special Consensus." Appendix B is an "Outline for Structural Analysis" or an outline of the previous outline.

Three years later, in 1971, the second work of the Castaneda series was published. This book, <u>A Separate Reality, Further Conversations With Don Juan</u>, implied itself to be a continuation of the first book. Acknowledging that the first book had reported an end to the *learnings*, it was not an easy task to have a reader believe that the *teachings* would not end, regardless. The way around this little problem of being too definite on the narrator's part was for the *author* to come up with a slight retraction for the voice of the narrator. At the end of the introduction to <u>A Separate Reality</u>, Carlos writes:

"At the time of my withdrawal I was convinced that my decision was final; I did not want to see Don Juan ever again. However, in April of 1968 an early copy of my book was made available to me and I felt compelled to show it to him. I paid him a visit. Our links of teacher-apprentice was mysteriously re-established, and I can say that on that occasion I began a second cycle of apprenticeship, very different from the first."[26]

The cycle was not all that different but perhaps more advanced. Don Juan was still the same old Indian but he was more relaxed and seemed more sympathetic to Carlos' plight. Drugs were still an important part of the teachings, but there were some additional points of emphasis, namely learning to *see* and learning to use the *will*.

Carlos was still the anthropologist; in fact, he tells us that the reason the second cycle of teachings

---

[26] Carlos Castaneda, <u>A Separate Reality: Further Conversations with Don Juan</u> (New York: Simon and Schuster, 1971), p 7

began was that he was trying to accumulate evidence to support his conclusion that "a skillful sorcerer could bring forth the most specialized range of perception in his apprentice by simply manipulating social cues."[27] Much of the book still deals with drug-induced experiences, but, at least, the intellectual trend was toward a more philosophical explanation for what Carlos experienced.

The book is separated again into two sections. The first section is entitled "The Preliminaries of Seeing" and the second "The Task of Seeing." Both sections are divided into numbered chapters and many of the chapters are dated, although the dates appear within the text as opposed to heading the text as in The Teachings of Don Juan.

There are a number of new characters, most notably Don Genaro who remains as an individual of great importance throughout the rest of the series. In addition there is a greater quantity of non-

---

[27] Ibid, p 24

ordinary events that are produced without the aid of psychotropics and more emphasis is given to these events than in the past, although the narrator is still convinced that the use of drugs was "an indispensable pre-requisite" in the understanding of Don Juan's knowledge.

The book ends with an extraordinary non-drug, non-ordinary event involving the sight of Don Genaro whisking his body to the top of some distant mountains then disappearing. There is a white space[28] and an end-note conversation between Don Juan and Carlos and a comment by the narrator that brings the story to a different kind of close.

> *"My mind could no longer uphold my old ordinary criteria of what is real. However, all these speculations I had thus far engendered about the nature of reality had been mere intellectual manipulations; the proof was that under the pressure of Don Juan and Don Genaro's acts my mind had entered into an impasse."*[29]

---

[28] Ibid, p 232. A new device for the series that is introduced here.

[29] Ibid, p 262

Conditions of a Solitary Bird

Carlos is still the intellectual, but he is not *certain* any longer.

Finally, there is a brief epilogue, an unusual technical device in that it is not used again in any of the other three books. It is an extremely important literary instrument for it "ends" this particular book but with a conclusion that lacks internal definitiveness. That is, technically an epilogue signals finality, but, what is contained in this particular epilogue leaves some room for a progression.

Don Juan slowly walked around me. He seemed to be deliberating whether or not to say something to me. Twice he stopped and seemed to change his mind. "Whether or not you return is thoroughly unimportant," he finally said. "However, you now have the need to live like a warrior. You have always known that, now you are simply in the position of having to make use of something you disregarded before. But you had to struggle for this knowledge, it wasn't just given to you; it wasn't just handed down to you. You had to beat it out of yourself. Yet you're still a luminous being. You are still going to die like everyone else. I once told you that there's nothing to change in a luminous egg." He was quiet for a moment. I knew he was looking at me, but I avoided his eyes. "Nothing has really changed in you," he said.[30]

Carlos has gained something, "Knowledge," but nothing has been given to him. He is different and "now needs to live like a warrior," but he hasn't changed, for he is and has always been a luminous being. So ends the further conversations with Don Juan.

Only one year later a book entitled <u>Journey to Ixtlan</u> subtitled <u>The Lessons of Don Juan</u> is published. It is obvious that that slight whisper that the previous book's epilogue was not a "true" ending has proved to be a shout. The story here continues, but with a total change of emphasis and a dramatic development in writing style.

---

[30] <u>Ibid</u>, p 263

Conditions of a Solitary Bird

Journey to Ixtlan also begins with an introduction and an academic justification for continuing the writings. However, within the obligatory explanation of the anthropological methods, there is a statement in no uncertain terms that this book is somehow *different* from the previous two. Carlos admits that he has been thick-headed as everyone has been saying he was all along.

The effects of those psychotropics had been so bizarre and impressive that I was forced to assume that such states were the only avenue to communicating and learning what Don Juan was attempting to teach me...That assumption was erroneous.[31]

The tone is academic, but extremely *honest*. There seems to be a real desire on the narrator's part to explain what he is doing and why. There are a number of long passages that deal with complicated

---

[31] Carlos Castaneda, Journey to Ixtlan: The Lessons of Don Juan (New York: Simon and Schuster, 1972), p. vii.

philosophical propositions in a clear, concise manner and indeed lend themselves, as in no previous book of the series, to a real understanding of what it means to be and think as a sorcerer. Also, there is an acknowledgement by the narrator that the conversations are, at least partially, influenced by the author; "...I gathered voluminous notes. In order to render those notes readable and still preserve the dramatic unity of Don Juan's teachings, I had to edit them, but what I have deleted is, I believe, immaterial to the points I want to raise." Still the narrator contends that he is letting Don Juan's words speak for themselves.[32]

Also in the introduction, to further differentiate this book from the others, Carlos admits that the use of drugs was unnecessary in the comprehension of Don Juan's knowledge. He states, "It was simply my lack of sensitivity which had fostered their use."

---

[32] Ibid, p xiv

Conditions of a Solitary Bird

The first half of **Journey to Ixtlan,** we are told is all the non-drug information which was discarded from previous field notes:

"I discarded those parts of my field notes in my earlier notes because they did not pertain to the use of psychotropic plants. I have now rightfully reinstated them in the first seventeen chapters of this work. The last three chapters are the field notes covering the events culminating in my *stopping the world*."[33]

So, as with the last two books, Journey to Ixtlan is divided into two sections. Part one is entitled "Stopping the World" and part two "Journey to Ixtlan." Both sections are again divided into chapters, but in this case the chapters are titled as well. There is a mild attempt to continue the disguise of a journal for the work. Some chapters are dated within the text; others are headed by dates. There are some however that are not dated at all and of these, three separate chapters follow the events of the same day.

---

[33] Ibid, p xii

The main differences between this presentation and the previous two is that it is strongly implied that Carlos "gains membership" or becomes a sorcerer during the course of writing this book. However, the text itself ends on a vague note and it appears obvious that a fourth book will soon appear:

> "We are going to leave you here . . . do what you think is proper. The ally will be waiting for you at the edge of that plain." He pointed to a dark valley in the distance. "If you don't feel that it is your time yet, don't keep your appointment . . . nothing is gained by forcing the issue. If you want to survive you must be crystal clear and deadly sure of yourself. Don Juan walked away without looking at me, but Don Genaro turned a couple of times and urged me with a wink and a movement of his head to go forward. I looked at them until they disappeared in the distance and then I walked to my car and drove away. I knew that it was not my time, yet."[34]

Carlos was told in earlier teachings that he must wrestle with an ally or spirit helper and overpower it before he could rightfully call himself a sorcerer and claim membership. He tells us in the

---
[34] Ibid, p 268

Conditions of a Solitary Bird

introduction to Ixtlan that he *has* gained membership but this book ends without his having tackled the ally. Therefore, in 1974, it was no surprise, that the fourth book of the Don Juan series, Tales of Power was published. Carlos Castaneda received his doctorate for the book, Journey to Ixtlan;[35] and so in Tales of Power most of the pretense at being academic is dropped, and the result is that this book is by far the most "literary" of the four. There is no introduction as in the first three books of the series. In contrast, at the beginning of The Tales of Power, we find a poem written by San Juan de la Cruz, from *Dichos de luz Amor*. This time the book is divided into three sections and these sections are headed by chapter titles. There are few specific datings for the chapters. Chapter one establishes itself in time as "the autumn of 1971." Most of the other time

---

[35] The book Journey to Ixtlan is filled as Carlos Castaneda's dissertation under a different title, Sorcery: A description of the World. The only difference is a two-page introduction by Castaneda, to be found at the end of this thesis.

references are to hour of day rather than day of week or even month of the year.

Part one, entitled "A Witness to the Acts of Power" begins only a few months after <u>Journey to Ixtlan</u> leaves off. Don Genaro by this time is so much a part of the teachings that he seems an aspect of Don Juan's personality. In the first chapter, Carlos has an appointment with knowledge in the form of a moth. We later find out that the moth is the ally that he must tackle to meet the requirements of initiation.

Part two is called "The Tonal and the Nagual" and the seven chapters contained in this section deal in some way with the explanation of clarification of these two terms.[36]

One of the greater scenic innovations in this section is that Carlos finds Don Juan in Mexico City

---

[36] The term *nagual* corresponds to the Eastern philosophy's nirvana or nothingness in that the *nagual* is the indescribable, the place where power hovers. Everything that has a name, or can be named is the *nagual*.

According to Don Juan, these two elements make up the tonality of our existence as human beings.

Conditions of a Solitary Bird

dressed in a made-to-order suit rather than the poncho, khakis, and sandals we were accustomed to seeing him in. The "teachings" proceed in this populated setting until later chapters which bring us to part three, entitled "The Sorcerer's Explanation," which contains four chapters of its own. This is a fascinating and possibly the most crucial section to be found in any of the first four books. For here Carlos performs a number of the extraordinary feats that have been baffling him for the past thirteen years. And, although the story stretches the reader's imagination to the furthest limits, the sorcerer's explanation (the one we are given for all that's happening) makes a nearly successful attempt at making all that is described sound perfectly credible. We, as readers, are made to understand all that is happening in terms of a sorcerer's perception of the world. After thirteen years and four novels, the reader is forced to accept what he sees if viewed in this light. Human beings can dissolve themselves and turn into crows or crickets or coyotes or reappear in all their corporealness on other planets, but all this takes place in one's perception. When Carlos asks Don Juan if a sorcerer could go to the moon, Juan replies, "Of course he can . . . but he wouldn't be able to bring back a bag of rocks though."[37] That is one of the fourth book's great achievements; it puts all the other books of the series into the proper perspective, the sorcerer's perspective. And the other great accomplishment is making abstract ideas more concrete.

For years men have been discussing nirvana, the unknown, the indescribable. In Tales of Power Carlos describes how it's possible to release the binding force of life that holds those components together which make up an individual personality;

"I again had the sensation of being tossed, spinning, and falling down at a tremendous speed. Then I exploded. I disintegrated. Something in me gave out; it released something I had kept locked up all my life. I was thoroughly aware then that my secret reservoir had been tapped and that it poured

---

[37] Carlos Castaneda, Tales of Power (New York: Simon and Schuster, 1974) p 270

Conditions of a Solitary Bird

out unrestrainedly. There was no longer the sweet unity I call "me." There was nothing and yet that nothing was filled. It was not light nor darkness, hot or cold, pleasant or unpleasant. It was not that I moved or floated or was stationary; neither was I a single unit, a self, as I am accustomed to being. I was a myriad of selves which were all "me" a colony of separate units that had a special allegiance to one another and would join unavoidably to form one single awareness, my human awareness. It was not that I "knew" beyond a shadow of a doubt, because there was nothing I could have "known" with, but, all my single awareness "knew" that the "I," the "me," of my familiar world was a colony, a conglomerate of separate and independent feelings that had an unbending solidarity to one another. The unbending solidarity of my countless awarenesses, the allegiance that those parts had, for one another was my life force."[38]

The book's ending is almost an extended metaphor for the technique Carlos Castaneda has employed for four novels to entice the reader to purchase the next book in the series. It is a "cliff hanger," literally. For, the book closes on a cliff top as Carlos and Pablito (another apprentice) bound,

---

[38] Ibid, p 162

without Don Juan or Genaro's aid, over the precipice and into the lonely and mysterious world of sorcerers.

"Don Juan and Don Genaro stepped back and seemed to merge with the darkness. Pablito held my forearm and we said goodbye to each other. Then a strange urge, a force, made me run with him to the northern edge of the mesa. I felt his arm holding me as we jumped and then I was alone."[39]

The reader is left to assume that Carlos has indeed "gained membership" and that this self-propelled flight over the precipice turned out all right. Obviously "Carlos" survived at least long enough to narrate this book for "Castaneda." The door is being left open purposefully for the fifth book in the series. Many have maintained that if "Carlos" or "Castaneda" or both have indeed reached this transcendental level of understanding and have divorced themselves totally from the petty world of man that a fifth book is impossible. Indeed many wonder how Carlos could write Tales of

---

[39] Ibid, p 287

Conditions of a Solitary Bird

Power after jumping from that cliff as we are told in that final chapter. I believe however if one looks to the texts and follows the trends of development, not only in the writing style, but in the teachings themselves, it becomes clear that a fifth book is indeed a necessity.

As we have seen, even from these brief descriptions, the pattern of development has been very subtle. Any one of the books could be read alone and enjoyed. In fact, some say that Carlos simply retold his story in the first three books, changing emphasis slightly as the years progressed. And, after he got his Doctoral degree, he wrote Tales of Power totally as an allegorical slap in the face to all his detractors and admirers alike. I do not believe that this is the case. Certainly "Carlos" is a coyote sorcerer and a trickster, but he is still basing his story on a series of age-old truths. The teachings consist mainly of four issues. Carlos learns what it means to be a "sorcerer" for one, but he also learns what it means to be "a man of knowledge" and a "warrior" and also a "hunter." And each of these conditions--as the story progresses—becomes more strongly rooted in the other conditions. A warrior for instance must first be a hunter. A sorcerer must be a warrior, and a man of knowledge must be able to see the world from more than one perspective. The "other" perspective we learn, along with Carlos, is the only "other" one that our teacher, Don Juan, knows. This unique perspective of sorcery.

Another important, even vital bit of developmental information is that a man of knowledge has a ***predilection***. In Separate Reality Carlos asks Don Juan to explain this concept:

"I said that a man of knowledge has his own predilection; mine is just to 'see' and to know; others do other things."

"What other things for example?"
"Take Sacateca, he's a man of knowledge and his predilection is dancing. So he dances and knows."
"Is the predilection of a man of knowledge something he does in order to know?"

Conditions of a Solitary Bird

"Yes, that is correct."[40]

From the very beginning we are given clues that Carlos indeed has a predilection as well, and his predilection is writing. On the very first day of apprenticeship Don Juan calls attention to Carlos' incessant writing. "What are you doing in your pocket? . . . Are you playing with your whanger?"[41] Carlos was taking notes inside the pocket of his windbreaker so he would not disturb Don Juan. Both Juan and Genaro are constantly clowning about Carlos trying to learn sorcery by writing everything down.

In Separate Reality, Genaro sits on his head in a figurative gesture to point out the absurdity of Carlos' constant note taking. But Don Juan points out, "it doesn't matter . . .if you ever learn to 'see.' I suppose you must do it your own weird way."[42] On a number of occasions in later sequences Genaro

---

[40] Castaneda, A Separate Reality, p 11

[41] Castaneda, Journey to Ixtlan, p 5

[42] Castaneda, A Separate Reality, p 215

and Juan actually make sure that Carlos has his writing gear before they will say or do anything with him. In the last chapter of Tales of Power, Carlos writes:

Don Juan handed me my writing pad, but I did not feel like taking notes. We sat in a half circle with Don Juan and Don Genaro at the ends. "You started on the path of knowledge writing, and you will finish the same way? Don Juan said. All of them urged me to write, as if my writing were essential.[43]

Earlier in this book, Don Juan even calls Carlos' ability to take notes without concentrating an "act of sorcery." there is one point at which Juan actually mentions writing as the *predilection* of his apprentice.

Speculating about the amount of "creativity," in this chapter, "The Role of Carlos, Carlitos, and Castaneda the Author" the great question that arises from all of this is, *why did Carlos Castaneda*

---

[43] Castaneda, Tales of Power, p 275

Conditions of a Solitary Bird

"choose" this particular style of presentation? Why did he write four books instead of just one? One possible answer is that the whole thing is a truthful account of an actual apprenticeship. If that were the case, it would explain why Carlos knew as little about his subject as he said he did and why there were constantly new qualifications to previous teachings.

Some of Castaneda's detractors have rejected this possibility entirely and even suggest that the four books were planned as a series from the beginning. Richard DeMille suggests that the dedication in book one, "For Don Juan and those two persons who shared his sense of magical time with me" is actually a dedication to Juan, Genaro, and Pablito. Two of these people are not introduced until book two and in book one there are no other characters of importance (besides Juan and Carlos) except for La Catalina, and it is most unlikely that she would be one of those "other two" since she allegedly tried to kill Carlos.

Also, this whole idea seems remarkable on one level since DeMille spends most of his time in his own book "proving" that none of these three people even exist. On another level, it seems perfectly feasible, however. Castaneda, it was shown earlier, is not reluctant to alter dates and juggle history a bit. It could be that many of the events that were recorded in later books actually took place even before the writing of book one in the series.

Any good sorcerer and warrior who is living out his predilection for writing and is trying to live impeccably in the academic world of university students might conceive the idea of writing down some of his apprenticeship in dissertation form to accomplish the magical feat of conjuring up a Ph.D.

It certainly does not appear that Castaneda was trying for a bestseller with the first book. The Teachings is too final and too separate from the rest of the series. The writing is too dry and the structural analysis, which takes up the entire second half of the book, hardly makes for enjoyable

Conditions of a Solitary Bird

bedtime reading. Also, one usually does not publish at a university press if shooting for sales of a million. Then, who are those "other two" of the dedication? I do not feel that it would be too difficult to accept that the dedication was made out of simple, courteous respect for "any" two individuals who may have assisted Carlos (in a myriad of possible ways) while he was conducting initial interviews. Within the text, it is made clear that Carlos did not stay with Don Juan the whole time he was making the original commitments to the arduous life of a warrior and sorcerer's apprentice.

Many of the chapters of the first three books begin and end with Carlos coming from or going to a number of unspecified places. Was Carlos being shifty or evasive by not being specific about his activities when he was not in the company of Don Juan, or did he feel that these activities simply did not pertain to the subject at hand? That is the question only Carlos could answer and I don't see why he would bother at this point. [author's update: Carlos Castaneda died April 27, 1998].

If indeed the dedication was made to two friends other than Pablito or Genaro, two likely candidates would probably be those mentioned in the introduction to The Teachings of Don Juan:

> *I was driving at night in the company of two Indian friends when I saw an animal that seemed to be a dog crossing the highway . . . talking excitedly, my friends agreed that it was a very unusual animal, and one of them suggested that it might be a diablero.*[44]

The reasons that I feel that these two friends are the ones of the dedication deal with a purely subjective observation that these are the only two friends who are not named in some way and are also the only two that Carlos mentions as being with him in any other capacity as "informants."

The possibility will always remain that the books were fictional constructions from the outset, in which case, Carlos Castaneda must be admired

---

[44] Castaneda, Teachings of Don Juan, p 3

for his courage to attempt such a hoax to merely circumvent the system and obtain a Ph.D. degree. It would certainly have been simpler and surer to have done what he said he had set out to do and write a scholarly "paper" on medicinal herbs. Indeed, if he was planning the endeavor as a financial scheme one must admire his foresight in predicting how the public would respond to a book published in a limited edition by a university press, and in predicting too that the response would not be totally negative to the second and third books of the series which contained retractions of main issues of the previous books.

My conclusion, therefore, is that the books were not "planned" from the beginning as a tetralogy. It is more likely that the books were left open-ended because they were factual accounts to a large degree. However, it could be that Castaneda, from a literary-financial perspective realized that he'd made a tactical error in The Teachings of Don Juan when he vowed there would be no more writing about his apprenticeship. The following books were always "complete." The reader always knew that as long as Carlos did not actually function in the world of sorcerers as a sorcerer, there would continue to be a story to be told. Now that he has allegedly "gained membership" the question still remains, will readers be as enthralled by the doings of a full-fledged sorcerer as they were by the bumbling apprentice?

We will have a short wait for our answer, for book five is destined to appear sometime near the beginning of 1978.[45] As long as Carlos Castaneda lives, I believe there will be a story to tell and one that will capture the reader. I think "someone" was trying to give the reader some insight of this account at the end of Tales of Power with these words:

"At this point a teacher would usually say to his disciple that they have arrived at a final

---

[45] Research for this thesis was completed before The Second Ring of Power was published, making this comment somewhat dated.

Conditions of a Solitary Bird

crossroad . . . to say such a thing is misleading though. In my opinion, there is no final crossroad, no final step to anything. And since there is no final step to anything, there shouldn't be any secrecy about any part of our lot as luminous beings."[46]

If the teachings were believed by Carlos—whether he made up the bulk or all of them or not-- and he follows the path of his predilection, there should be no final crossroads for him and no final books.

---

[46] Castaneda, Tales of Power, p 227

Gordon Richiusa

Conditions of a Solitary Bird

4. TRACING PERSONAL HISTORY
CHARACTER DEVELOPMENT OF THE MAIN CHARACTERS

"What did you call your father," I asked.

"I called him Dad," he said with a very serious face.

"What did you call your mother,?" I asked.

"I called her mom," he replied in a naive tone.[47]

Let us now begin to sort out the pertinent biographical information about his main characters that can be obtained from the Castaneda texts. We will be tracing their personal histories and applying what we learn to their development as characters in the story. The body of this section will treat the most important characters most fully and the characters of lesser importance according to their varying degrees of impact, not only on the other characters, but on the reader as well. Therefore, the

---

[47] Carlos Castaneda, Journey to Ixtlan: The Lessons of Don Juan (New York: Simon and Schuster, 1972) p 10

characters of Don Juan Matus and Don Cenaro will be dealt with in depth while other characters may be only mentioned or ignored entirely.

The epigraph quoted above, from Journey to Ixtlan, points out the difficulty one encounters when trying to piece together a biographical chart for the illusive old Indian. Don Juan, simply did not have too much to say about his personal history, even when Carlos was interested. "I don't have personal history anymore," he told the inquisitive anthropologist. "I dropped it one day when I felt it was no longer necessary."

The erasure of one's past life, in fact, was an important condition for acquiring an understanding of Don Juan's knowledge. And later, when Don Juan became more amenable about relinquishing historical data, Carlos too had acquired a love for the mysterious and stopped his old mentor from revealing those little bits of history that every reader longed to know. "I did not want Don Juan to tell me about himself. He paused as if he had read my mind."[48] At times it almost appears as if Carlos and Juan are conspiring to conceal important facts; luckily, however, both have moments of human weakness and make mistakes. The facts that leak out here and there can be, and are here, organized into a brief sketch of Don Juan's personal history. Don Juan was born in the "Southwest" of the North American continent in 1891. He spent nearly all of his life in Mexico. In 1900 his family was exiled by the Mexican government to Central Mexico along with thousands of other Sonoran Indians. He lived in Central and Southern Mexico until 1940,[49] when he moved to Arizona. Sometime during the middle or late 1960's, Juan Matus moved his residence back to Mexico. We know only that his home was somewhere in the state of Sonora, along the Pan-American highway[50] in an area that was a few days

---

[48] Ibid, p 267

[49] Castaneda, The Teachings of Don Juan: A Yaqui Way of Knowledge (New York: Ballantine Books, Inc., 1969) p 96

[50] Castaneda, Journey to Ixtlan, p 140

walk from both a volcanic mountain range[51] and the U.S. border.

When he was seven years old, his mother was killed during the Yaqui wars with the Mexican government. He watched the event.

What I remember the most is the terror and sadness that fell upon me when the Mexican soldiers killed my mother . . . she was a poor and humble Indian. Perhaps it was better that her life was over then. I wanted to be killed with her, because I was a child. But the soldiers picked me up and beat me. When I grabbed onto my mother's body, they hit my fingers with a horsewhip and broke them. I didn't feel any pain, but I couldn't grasp anymore, and then they dragged me away.[52]

Later his father also died from wounds received in this battle. Juan survived on his own by shining

---

[51] Ibid, p 201

[52] Castaneda, A Separate Reality: Further Conversations with Don Juan (New York: Simon and Schuster, 1971)

shoes and eating scraps off tables at restaurants. Later he sold medicinal herbs in the marketplace in Oaxaca with his friend Don Vicente Medrano. When he was in his late 20's or early 30's, he "killed a man with a single blow of his arm."[53] A short time before he met Carlos, Juan had acquired a reputation for drinking a great deal[54] but the evidence in the books suggests that if he did drink alcohol, he has now given it up completely. There is even evidence that he will not drink now even if alcohol is offered to him:

"I passed the bottle and everyone poured himself a small drink, everyone except Don Juan; he just took the bottle and placed it in front of Lucio, who was at the end of the line."[55]

Lucio is Juan's one living grandson, the offspring of Eulalio, Juan's son. Eulalio died as a

---

[53] Castaneda, The Teachings of Don Juan, p 96

[54] Castaneda, Journey to Ixtlan, p 7-8

[55] Castaneda, A Separate Reality, p 59

young man and Don Juan was witness to this death too:

> *"Take my son Eulalio . . . he was crushed by rocks while working in the construction of the Pan-American highway . . . when I came to the blasting area he was almost dead, but his body was so strong that it kept moving and kicking . . . never again would I look at his fine figure pacing the Earth."*[56]

There is no mention in the books of a wife for Juan or of her death. The only other living relative that he has, or Carlos has written about, is his daughter-in-law who takes care of him when he dislocates his ankle.[57]

Don Juan apparently lived for many years as a respected Brujo and member of a Yaqui community, but has since disassociated himself from his kind, to the injury of his reputation. "He was a real sorcerer once," Benigno added. "I mean a real one. My folks

---

[56] Ibid, p 90

[57] Castaneda, The Teachings of Don Juan, p 61

say he was the best. But he took to peyote and became a nobody."[58]

Juan still, however, is a character that has earned apparently some kind of respect, although he no longer performs any cultural function as a curer.

Bill, the character who introduced Don Juan and Carlos, mentions a kind of reverence the Indians of Juan's area give to him. "The Indians around here know him, yet they never mention him. And that's something."[59] Carlos talks about an early search for the "eccentric Mexican Indian's" house and the feeling that the Indians whom they had asked for directions had deliberately misled them.

After giving up the life of yerbero (or herb seller) and curer, Juan apparently has supported himself at least partly, with the returns from some undefined financial stock.[60]

---

[58] Castaneda, A Separate Reality, p 69

[59] Ibid, p 3

[60] Castaneda, Tales of Power (New York: Simon and Schuster, 1974) p 162

This summary-biography includes most of what we know about Don Juan's personal history. Everything else one must surmise purely from what is implied as fact, For instance, Juan Matus possibly could possess some kind of formal education, for we know him to speak "flawless Spanish." As a stockholder, we know he prefers to dress in tailored-to-order suits and we must assume that his business is important enough to him to move to Mexico City from Sonora for, at least, short periods of time to accomplish business tasks. It is likely too, knowing Juan's love for achieving impeccability at all social levels, that he has another residence in Mexico City quite unlike the one described in Separate Reality[61] a wattle-and-daub, thatched-roofed hut of one room with bundles of herbs and strangely contorted, dry medicinal roots hanging from the walls and a single kerosene lantern hanging from a wooden beam.

It is easy to see the familiar khaki and poncho attired Juan in such a setting, but we can only

---

[61] Castaneda, A Separate Reality, p 189

assume he is housed otherwise when dressed in his three-piece suits. In fact, it is strange just how easy to picture he is for the reader, for there are almost no real descriptions of his figure for us. We see him only as "a white-haired old Indian" in Teachings of Don Juan who "though his dark face and neck were wrinkled, showing his age . , . his body was agile and muscular."[62] In Separate Reality the first meeting is again described and Don Juan's figure is fleshed out just a bit more.

> *"The Indian was of medium height. His hair was white and short, and grew a bit over his ears, accentuating the roundness of his head. He was very dark; the deep wrinkles on his face gave him the appearance of age, yet his body seemed to be strong and fit. I watched him for a moment. He moved around with a nimbleness that I would have thought impossible for an old man."*[63]

Don Juan does not fit the stereotypical view of the elderly, however. He was, according to the dates given in the Castaneda text, more than 77 years old

---

[62] Castaneda, The Teachings of Don Juan, p 1

[63] Castaneda, A Separate Reality, p 1-2

when we first met him in the **Teachings of Don Juan**. Simple computation reveals his age at close to 90 in **Tales of Power,** and what is remarkable is how little Juan changes in all the time we

know him. In fact, he is probably one of the most consistent characters in the Castaneda tetralogy, if not in all literature. Thirteen years passed, but he never gets any older, or less strong. Carlos gains and loses weight. He matures and his writing style develops, but Juan's narrative oratorical style never alters. He is consistent in tone, voice and dramatic style. This is not to say that he is monotonous. Far from it. From the beginning we never know what to expect from him, in act or word. Juan is predictably unpredictable. Carlos comments on the possible reasons for his teacher's bizarre behavior.

As a rule, he always concluded each of our sessions on an abrupt note; thus the dramatic tone of the ending tone of each chapter is not a literary device of my own, it was a device proper of Don

Conditions of a Solitary Bird

Juan's oral tradition. It seemed to be a mnemonic device that helped me to retain the dramatic quality and importance of the lessons.[64]

Of course, also, to be unpredictable or "without routines" was a condition that a warrior and sorcerer needed to fulfill. Juan fulfills this condition particularly well.

He is continually popping up when he is least expected. Here are two representative passages:

1) "Hello, hello! Look who's here!" someone said, tapping me lightly on the shoulder. The voice and the touch made me jump. I quickly turned to my right. My mouth opened in surprise. The person who had spoken to me was Don Juan.
"My God, Don Juan! I exclaimed and a shiver shook my body from head to toe. "What are you doing here?"[65]
2) I parked my car and walked a short distance to the house. To my surprise, I found him there. "Don Juan! I didn't expect to find you here," I said.[66]

---

[64] Ibid, p 8

[65] Castaneda, Tales of Power, p 105

[66] Ibid, p 11

Don Juan does show some human qualities, weaknesses that he calls "his own peculiar way of indulging." The greatest example of Don Juan's indulgence is when he is sad. One of the things that seems to make him sad is the plight of the Indians. "We Indians have nothing," Don Juan tells Carlos in Separate Reality. "All you see around here belongs to the Yoris.[67] The Yaquis have only their wrath and what the land offers to them freely."

Another source of sadness for Juan is the sadness that all sorcerers must feel as individuals who have separated themselves from their pasts, their homes and their feelings as men. Don Genaro discusses his metaphorical striving to regain his past has his "Journey to Ixtlan," the place of his home.

I will never reach Ixtlan," he said. His voice firm but soft, almost a murmur. "Yet in my feelings. . . sometimes I think I am just one step from reaching it. Yet I never will. In my journey I don't even find the familiar landmarks I used to know. Nothing is any longer the same." Don Juan and Don Genaro looked at each other. There was something so sad

---

[67] Yoris, an Indian term meaning "Mexican".

about their look. "In my journey to Ixtlan find only phantom travelers," he said softly.[68]

Juan realizes his sadness and the sources of it, yet to be an impeccable warrior does not mean that he cannot have human feelings but only that he cannot let these feelings govern him by becoming obsessions: "Don Juan was right again when he said that a warrior could not avoid pain and grief, but only the indulging in them."[69]

Human emotion indeed is an important enough part of being a warrior that in the outline for the system of beliefs, which govern the condition an antidote for the loneliness that could result from this self-imposed "aloneness" is integrated into the system:

"Only if one loves this earth with unbending passion can one release one's sadness . . . a warrior is always joyful because his love is unalterable and his beloved, the earth, embraces him and bestows upon him inconceivable gifts. The sadness belongs

---

[68] Castaneda, Journey to Ixtlan, p 264

[69] Castaneda, Tales of Power, p 281

only to those who hate the very thing that gives shelter to their beings . . . this lovely being, which is alive to its last recesses and understands every feeling, soothed me, it cured me of my pains, and finally when I had fully understood my love for it, it taught me freedom...without an unwavering love for the being that gives you shelter, aloneness is loneliness."[70]

The final aspect of Don Juan's character that I wish to deal with here is his sense of humor. Carlos tries to convince the reader that Don Juan "develops" a more frequent use of humor as the series progresses. In the second book, <u>A Separate Reality</u>, he writes of the initiation of the second cycle of apprenticeship as being "very different from the first.

"The total mood of Don Juan's teachings was more relaxed. He laughed and also made me laugh a great deal. There seemed to be a deliberate intent on his part to minimize seriousness in general. He clowned during the truly crucial moments of this second cycle, and thus helped me to overcome experiences, which could easily have become obsessive. His premise was that a light and

---

[70] <u>Ibid</u>, p 286

Conditions of a Solitary Bird

amenable disposition was needed in order to withstand the impact and the strangeness of the knowledge he was teaching me."[71]

Whatever Don Juan's reasons for his use of humor, and lightness to establish the teachings, they are not "the new development" that the above statement implies, It is true, perhaps, that Don Juan is more serious and forcefully didactic in the first book than the second; however, if we take Castaneda's chronology as valid, then the incidents in the first half of the third book must be taken into account. Don Juan therefore emerges as consistent as ever. As I have already pointed out in chapter two, on the very first day of the apprenticeship he inquired about Carlos' taking notes on a small pad in the pocket of his windbreaker, "What are you doing in your pocket? Are you playing with your whanger?"[72]

---

[71] Castaneda, A Separate Reality, p 7

[72] Castaneda, Journey to Ixtlan, p 5

The sequence just before this is a twist on an old story that Don Juan constructs for Carlos to show him how preposterous his preparations have been for their meeting:

I had heard the theme of the story before. It had to do with Jews in Germany and the way one could tell who was a Jew by the way they pronounced certain words. I also knew the punch-line: The young man was going to get caught because the official had forgotten the key word and had asked him how to pronounce another word which was very similar but which the young man had not learned to say correctly. Don Juan seemed to be waiting for me to ask what happened, so I did.

"What happened to him?" I asked, trying to sound naive and interested in the story.

"The young man, who was truly foxy . . . realized that the official had forgotten the key word, and before the man could say anything else he confessed that he had prepared himself for six months." . . .this time he had turned the tables on me. The young man's confession was a new element and I no longer knew how the story would end. "Well, what happened then?" I asked, truly interested. "The young man was killed instantly, of course," he said and broke into a roaring laughter.[73]

The way Don Juan changes the story and entraps Carlos' interest is reminiscent of Feste's wordplay with Olivia in <u>Twelfth Night</u>, or any of a number of exchanges between Lear's Fool and the king. Shakespeare, indeed knew the value of the "fool" as a tool for biting commentary and as a mouthpiece for wisdom as well as humor. Castaneda seems to draw the character of his <u>brujo</u> from the same stock.

Historically comedians have been dealt with as divine or magical characters and Carl Jung went so far as to outline similarities between the clown and shamans.

It is at this point that we should turn our attention to the discussion of Don Genaro as a

---

[73] <u>Ibid</u>, p 4

character in Castaneda's tetralogy, for it is around him that the incidents, both most frightening and most hilarious seem to revolve.

Don Genaro's appearance in <u>Separate Reality</u> came just under halfway through this novel and with him an element in the series which could be described as "pure magic." He was a character kept in reserve by the author for the special or transcendental occasion. He was very Don-Juanian in some respects, but he seemed to epitomize certain characteristics almost as Hyde was made to epitomize certain of the evil characteristics of Dr. Jekyl.

To get a picture of Juan's and Genaro's similarities and differences and the way they play off one another in the text, I will here do for Genaro what l did for Juan at the beginning of this chapter and gather together what we know about him in the form of a brief semi-biography.

Conditions of a Solitary Bird

Don Genaro appeared in chapter six of a Separate Reality[74] as an even more mysterious character than Don Juan Matus; for he was simply a first name and remained as such throughout the rest of the series, in spite of the fact that his importance to and direct involvement with Carlos' indoctrination mushrooms with each new encounter. From the beginning, the literary treatment of Genaro is different from that of the other sorcerers. We are told, for instance, that Carlos had "already made his acquaintance, although very briefly" but that nothing out of the ordinary had occurred. Carlos goes so far as to say that "I had not really looked at him at that time, except in a glancing fashion."[75] Genaro is presented as a sorcerer from the beginning and what makes this lackluster first encounter remarkable is the fact that all of the sorcerers that Carlos had met up to this time were, at least, impetus for an experience that was "non-

---

[74] Castaneda, A Separate Reality, p 92

[75] Ibid, p 92

ordinary." When Carlos met Sacateca[76] he experienced a feeling of faintness or numbness when Sacateca tapped his toe behind his heel in a fashion that Don Juan called "a dance." When Carlos dropped in on, Don Vicente[77] he was given some "power plants"[78] and encountered his allies.

Carlos' first meeting with Don Genaro is so unremarkable that we as readers hear of it only as an afterthought. And then, in the next sentence there is another strange development. Genaro is described:

...I had had the feeling he was as old as Don Juan. As he stood at the door of his house, however, I noticed that he was definitely younger. He was perhaps in his early He was shorter than Don Juan and slimmer, very dark and wiry. His hair was thick and graying and a bit long; it ran over his ears and forehead. His face was round and hard. A very

---

[76] Castaneda, A Separate Reality, p 14

[77] Ibid, p 30-34

[78] Power plants, a term usually applied to plants with hallucinogenic properties, but refers in general to any plant used to benefit a sorcerer.

Conditions of a Solitary Bird

prominent nose made him look like a bird of prey with small dark eyes.[79]

We do not know Genaro's age with any more exactitude than Carlos' conjecture. We know only that he lives in Central Mexico, that his home was once in Ixtlan, and that he calls himself a member of the Mazatec tribe. We can locate his home roughly from a statement made in Tales of Power,[80] but our calculations will leave us in the midst of several Mexican states. At least with Don Juan we know he is in Sonora. With Genaro we can only guess, and with no more information than is given one must truly be a sorcerer to "see" the locality of his home correctly.

Genaro's similarities to a clown are apparent from the beginning. His laughter is so continuous, however, that there is no need for a painted on smile. When he greets Carlos at his home, "His

---

[79] Castaneda, A Separate Reality, p 93

[80] Castaneda, Tales of Power, p 282

words were a polite formula I had heard before in various rural areas of Mexico. Yet as he said the words he laughed joyously for no overt reason."

From here on it is almost one continuous circus of laughs for Genaro. He laughs at Carlos' writing and laughs at Carlos' fear of death, then he "sits" on his head, without the aid of his arms or hands to the utter bewilderment of Carlos and again laughs at Carlos because Carlos is bewildered.

Genaro, in the midst of his laughter, is not just a clown. He is merely a light-hearted version of Don Juan. Juan is occasionally light; Cenaro is occasionally serious.

Juan talks endlessly to his pupil; Genaro's predilection is not to talk but to act. Don Juan very seriously tells Carlos to be careful when listening to Genaro because "although what he says is funny it is not a joke."

Don Genaro gave a description of what he called "the arrangement of the other world" and

Conditions of a Solitary Bird

how a teacher could show each layer of the world to his students.

You start at the very bottom and then your teacher takes you with him in his flight and soon, boom! You go through the first layer, then a little while later, boom! You go through the second; and boom! You go through the third ...[81]

This is the first time that Genaro has spoken at any length and Carlos' and Juan's reactions to this outburst are made obvious and immediate.

Don Genaro took me through ten booms to the last layer of the world. When he had finished talking Don Juan looked at me and smiled knowingly. "Talking is not Genaro's predilection . . . but if you care to get a lesson, he will teach you about the equilibrium of things." Don Genaro nodded affirmatively; he puckered up his mouth and closed his eyelids halfway. I thought his gesture was delightful.[82]

---

[81] Castaneda, A Separate Reality, p 99

[82] Ibid, p 99

Don Juan's statement, Genaro's gesture, and Carlos' over-reaction to these simple movements are symbolic of the relation of the three for the rest of the series.

Juan is the voice of the philosophies and techniques; Genaro is the body. Carlos' tonal responds to Juan and his nagual responds to Genaro. From the moment Genaro takes Carlos clumsily through the ten layers of the world, his speeches become fewer but his acts become greater, both in number and impact. The lesson on the "equilibrium of things" is, without a doubt, the most intriguing, dramatic and descriptive scene in the second book. Genaro takes Carlos (and his own two apprentices, Nestor and Pablito) to the bottom of a waterfall. The description of the terrain is one of the best literal scenic descriptions that we have had up to this point:

Directly above us there was a huge, dark, bluish cloud that looked like a floating roof; it had a well defined edge and was shaped like an enormous half circle. To the west, on the high mountains of the

Conditions of a Solitary Bird

Cordillera Central, the rain seemed to be descending on the slopes. It looked like a whitish curtain falling on the green peaks. To the east there was the long, deep valley; there were only scattered clouds over the valley and the sun was shining there. The contrast between these two areas was magnificent.[83]

Even with the seeming "impersonal" description of the area Castaneda seems to be establishing contrasts between dark and light, storm and calm and perhaps Genaro and Juan. Without a word Genaro proceeds to climb the sheer side of the waterfall cliff and performs a series of remarkable acrobatics on the cliff face.

He threw his arms up suddenly, lifted his head, and flipped his body swiftly in a sort of lateral somersault to his left. The boulder where he had been standing was round and when he jumped he disappeared behind it.[84]

---

[83] Ibid, p 99

[84] Ibid, p 99

Later it is Juan, not Genaro who explains the feat. Genaro's powers affect Carlos' body in ways that defy physics. Certainly Don Juan has baffled his pupil with acts of telepathy and clairvoyance, but it is Genaro whose gentle touch is able to cause physical agony in the narrator, and whose childish antics can cause Carlos to react with uncontrollable fear.

He began to move backwards, jumping on his seat, and went all the way to the end of the ramada and back . . . the sight of Don Genaro leaping backwards on his buttocks, instead of being funny as it should have been, threw me into an attack of fear so intense that Don Juan had to strike me repeatedly on the top of my head with his knuckles.[85]

By the fourth book, the symbols for the Genaro-Juan split are more frequent and obvious. When Carlos asks Genaro a question Don Juan answers. "I

---

[85] Castaneda, Tales of Power, p 55

asked Don Genaro what a double did, or what a sorcerer did with the double. Don Juan answered."[86]

When Juan speaks into Carlos' right ear, Genaro speaks simultaneously into his left.[87] The following quotation leaves little room for speculation. The narrator Carlos is not implying the closeness of the two characters any longer. He is telling us straight out.

"Don Juan and Don Genaro stopped and turned in unison; their eyes moved and focused on me with such uniformity and precision that they seemed to be one single person."[88]

Carlos may be trying to tell us also that Juan and Genaro are like traits in a personality; they get mixed up occasionally or at times one trait becomes dominant over the others, but in the final analysis there is always the allegiance that one personality trait has to the other. Perhaps all sorcerers are

---

[86] Ibid, p 52

[87] Ibid, p 183

[88] Ibid, p 274-275

unified in some way as with this realization of Carlos' in Tales of Power.

They were both such a strange unnerving mixture of Don Genaro and Don Juan . . I knew that Pablito and Nestor were using Don Genaro and Don Juan as models for behavior. I myself had found that I also was behaving more and more like them.[89]

And perhaps this unification could even relate back to the sequence in the later pages of Tales of Power where Carlos sees himself as a countless number of personality traits or "nuggets of awareness" that have an unbending solidarity for one another that is life itself.

One final bit of evidence for the case of the "parts making up the whole" is the relationship that "La Catalina," the only significant female character thus far in the entire series, has with the rest of the characters. La Catalina, aside from being a source for a balance of masculine-feminine traits is a

---

[89] Castaneda, Tales of Power, p 216

Conditions of a Solitary Bird

character worthy of note in that she is the only character, besides Juan and Carlos, discussed in all four of the books. She is the source of terror for Carlos, but also stirs emotions that the other main characters cannot. These emotions deal with the male-female attractions of sexuality. "I scrutinized her carefully and concluded that she was a beautiful woman."[90]

Carlos' encounters with her could even be deciphered as symbolic of the sexual act. His descriptions are imagistic, sensual; they deal with the senses, and at one point when he says he "was so close to her that I felt her clothes on my face" he takes a wild boar fore-leg and thrusts it "into her belly," as he is directed by Don Juan.[91]

Later we find out that Carlos could not have really hurt the sorceress, because she was too powerful, that she did not really want to kill him but was a friend of Don Juan's and was trying to help in

---

[90] Castaneda, Journey to Ixtlan, p 217

[91] Castaneda, A Separate Reality, p 210

the teachings, and that Genaro, not Juan is really Carlos' benefactor. It is one big sorcerer family, or sorcerer body. One trait becomes more important at times than others, but they are all united by the force called "the designs of power."

As tools for Castaneda, Genaro, Catalina, Juan and the rest all serve useful purposes. Our debt to Juan of course is greatest. Whether the books be fact or fiction or a combination of the two, we must be aware how fortunate Castaneda was to find a Don Juan to speak the philosophies and to have characters like Genaro and Catalina to portray what is spoken. If Carlos Castaneda had presented the ideas of these books as his own, with his own "voice" how few would have heard? Indeed, how few would have even listened? I must agree with Ronald Sukenich when he answers Joyce Carol Oates on the question of the books being works of art; "Ms. Oates, to answer your questions directly, these books are works of art, but works of art don't have to be novels."[92]

---

[92] Ronald Sukenich, "Upward and Juanward: The Possible Dream" in Daniel Noel, <u>Seeing Castaneda: Reactions to Don Juan, Writings of Carlos Castaneda</u> (New York: Capricorn Books, 1976 p 110-120

Gordon Richiusa

5. FROM PLATO TO JUANCHO

The philosophical viewpoints expressed in the four Castaneda volumes are intricate and complete enough that a thesis could easily be written from this single perspective. In this chapter, I will touch upon a few possible literary and philosophical precursors for what is expounded.

An over-riding concept in the sorcerer's teachings is the concept of "seeing" as opposed to "looking." When looking, an individual experiences the things of the world, usually with his eyes, according to his preconceptions of the reality of those things. When an individual "sees," however, he experiences the world with his whole being, including the usual physical senses and some undefined sensory receptor that is called "the will." When one "sees," therefore, one experiences the things of the world more fully and directly than if one is simply looking at those things. The result is that one experiences the "true reality" as opposed to simply the reality of social consensus.

This concept has a philosophical forerunner, perhaps, in a view expressed by Plato with his "universal forms." For Plato, in addition to every spatiotemporal entity there was also a "form" or non-spatial, non-temporal and non-perceptible entity that was the "true reality" of each entity. For every oak, pine or poplar there was the form "tree." Even in this highly simplified version of the Platonic description of universal "forms," similarities to the teachings of Don Juan can be seen.

Plato's idea of universal forms presupposes, in the end, a whole other world or "separate reality" that co-exists on a non-temporal plane with the reality of our senses. Don Juan takes this idea of universals a couple of steps further. For Juan, each individual entity can be perceived in a different way from that of sense-perception. But these forms are not fixed, but rather more "alive" and changing than

Conditions of a Solitary Bird

our perception of them. This conversation from Separate Reality may shed some light on this distinction:

"Do things look consistently the same every time you 'see' them?"

"Things don't change. You change your way of looking, that's all."

"I mean, Don Juan, that if you 'see' for instance, the same tree, does it remain the same everytime you see it?

"No, ilt changes and yet it is the same."

"But if the same tree changes everytime you 'see' it, your 'seeing' may be a mere illusion."

"When you learn to 'see' . . . a thing is never the same every time you 'see' it, and yet it is the same. I told you, for instance, that a man is like an egg. Everytime I 'see' the same man I 'see' an egg, it is not the same egg."[93]

Juan later makes this definition more nearly complete when he explains that things are composed of fibers of light and that one may tell how a man, for instance, is feeling (sick, healthy, angry, sad, etc.) by the color and intensity of his

---

[93] Carlos Casteneda, <u>A Separate Reality: Further Conversations with Don Juan</u> (New York: Simon and Schuster, 1971) p 31

luminous fibers. This idea is comparable to the ideas of auras and goes back perhaps to the biblical belief that divine beings had halos of light that could be perceived around their heads.

William Blake made a distinction like that of Don Juan's in the final lines of his Vision of the Last Judgement:

"When the sun rises do you not see a round disc of fire somewhat like a guinea?" O, no no no, I see an innumerable company of the heavenly host crying "Holy Holy Holy is the Lord Cod Almighty;" I question a window concerning a sight. I look through it and not with it.

Much has been made of the similarities between Zen Buddhist teachings and those of the Yaqui sorcerer.[94] Carlos Castaneda has vehemently opposed any comparison of the two perspectives, but I think a strong enough case has been made that

---

[94] James Boyd, "The Teachings of Don Juan from a Buddist Perspective," Christian Century, March 28 1978, p 360-363; Gwyneth Cravens, "The Arc of Flight", Harpers Magazine, September 1974, p 43

Conditions of a Solitary Bird

I will here examine some of those similarities, "imagined" or not.

We have already discussed, in part, the likeness that the Buddhist concept of nirvana has to the sorcerer's feat of experiencing the nagual by loosening the ties that the individual component parts have for one another. This journey into the unspeakable or indefinable as described by Carlos in Tales of Power is similar also to the concept that is at the core of Buddhist dharmic analysis.

Basically, dharmic analysis is the technique for "reversing the wheel of life" or undoing the rigid limitations of normal perception. James W. Boyd describes the technique's basic assertions:

...This is an extension of the type of analysis . . . which analyzes "self" and "body" into component parts. Critically examining each of the so-called parts of the phenomenal world, the Buddhist discovers that all phenomena initially supposed to be real, are in fact a combination of still smaller "parts" which in turn are simply abstractions for other units. As the analysis continues beyond the empirical realm, a theory of the "atomic" structures of all phenomena results. All phenomena are made

up of dharmas (atomic units). Even the dharmas, however, are not substantial self-existents; rather, they too are designations for a composite of smaller, conditioned and interdependent parts (pratitya samutpada). All phenomena appear to be empty of any identifiable permanent essence.[95]

We need not return again at any length to a comparison of Buddhism and Castaneda's idea of the "parts making up the whole"; the reader of this thesis will be able to make this connection himself. The purpose of both these techniques is the restructuring of the practitioner's view of the world.

Taoists and Zen Buddhists use a different technique for acquiring this new description, and this too finds its American Indian counterpart in the teachings of Don Juan. The Taoist's and Zen Buddhist's attempt to undo the world by tuning into natural phenomena which one does not usually consider. Classic examples are the contemplation of the "hole" in the middle of a wheel rather than the spokes of the wheel discs; or centering ones

---

[95] Boyd, p 362

attention on the "emptiness" of a bowl rather than the container's outward structure.

Both the method of dharmic analysis and the Tao-Zen techniques for acquiring a new perception of the world seem to be portrayed at some level in the book Journey to Ixtlan. Don Juan tells Carlos that he is going to teach the apprentice "not-doing" and instructs his disciple to proceed to meditate on a small pebble placed on a large boulder. Don Juan's first directive is to focus on the unusual details to reduce the world and in so doing eventually enlarge it. At another point, Juan tells Carlos to focus on the shadows of the leaves in a tree rather than the leaves on the branches.

The details of the porous rock, in the small area where my eyes were focused were so vivid and so precisely defined that the top of the round peak became a vast world for me; and yet it was really a reduced vision of the rock.[96]

---

[96] Carlos Castaneda, Journey to Ixtlan: The Lessons of Don Juan (New York: Simon and Schuster, 1971) p 198

At another point, Don Juan tells Carlos to focus on the shadows between the leaves on a single branch of a tree, rather than the leaves or the branches. This exercise is done to gain a new view of the world and is remarkably like Tao-Zen techniques called <u>wei-wu-wei</u> or action in non-action discussed above.

The Zen methodology for communicating this philosophy has a number of other parallels with the methods of Juan, as can be found in a book by Eugen Herrigel called <u>Zen in the Art of Archery</u>. This "true story," originally published in the U.S. in 1953, is a first person account, which deals with a philosophy professor's strivings to learn the illusive philosophy of Zen. While teaching in Japan, Eugen Herrigel apprenticed himself to an archery master, with no preconceptions as to how the training would proceed or the real reasons for it. He, like Castaneda, was one of the first Westerners to break through tradition and learn an esoteric teaching. He, like Castaneda, struggles, fails, gives up, struggles

Conditions of a Solitary Bird

some more and eventually attains his goal. He is taught, as is Castaneda, by a master who is both tricky and articulate. He, like Castaneda, engages in long question and answer sessions with his teacher, has his teacher perform impossible tasks, is worked mercilessly, and learns a method for restructuring the world called "not-doing." This term is actually employed by Herrigel and though I am not trying to say that Castaneda stole (consciously or unconsciously) this term from Herrigel the similarities of the two books (which are more numerous than those mentioned) are cause enough for examination by some student of philosophy at a later date. Here I'd like to point out one more parallel between the teaching methods employed in Zen and by Juan and draw my comparison from quotations in Herrigel's book and one from the Journey to Ixtlan.

In the introduction to Journey to Ixtlan, Don Juan delineates a strategy for Carlos as to how a friend of the narrator should proceed to change the actions of his rebelious nine year-old son. The plan seemed much like the tactics Don Juan had employed with Carlos for the ten years of the apprenticeship.

I was to instruct my friend to have the man (a hired skidrow bum) follow him or wait for him at a place where he would go with his son. The man, in response to a pre-arranged cue to be given after any objectionable behavior on the part of the child, was supposed to leap from a hiding place, pick the child up and spank the living daylights out of him. "After the man scares him, your friend must help the little boy regain his confidence, in any way he can. If he follows this procedure three or four times I assure you that that child will feel differently towards everything. He will change his idea of the world."[97]

In <u>Zen and the Art of Archery</u> Herrigel, in explanation of the Zen teaching methods, presents

---

[97] <u>Ibid</u>, p xi

Conditions of a Solitary Bird

an anecdote from D. T. Suzuki's book <u>Zen Buddhism and its Influences on Japanese Culture:</u>[98]

> *The Japanese fencing master sometimes uses the Zen method of training. Once, when a disciple came to a master to be disciplined in the art of fencing, the master, who was in retirement in his mountain hut, agreed to undertake the task. The pupil was made to help him gather wood for kindling, draw water from a nearby spring, split wood, make the fire, cook rice, sweep the rooms and garden, and generally look after his household affairs. There was no regular or technical teaching in the art. After some time, the young man was dissatisfied, for he had not come to work as a servant to the old gentleman, but to learn the art of swordsmanship. So one day he approached the master and asked him to teach him. The master agreed. The result was that the young man could not do any piece of work with any feeling of safety. For when he began to cook rice early in the morning, the master would appear and strike him from behind with a stick. When he was in the midst of his*

---

[98] Eugen Herrigel, <u>Zen in the Art of Archery</u> (New York: Vintage Books, 1971) p 7-8

sweeping, he would be feeling the same blow from somewhere, from an unknown direction. He had no peace of mind; he had to be always on the qui vive. Some years passed before he could successfully dodge the blow from whatever source it might come. But the master was not satisfied with him yet. One day the master was found cooking his vegetables over an open fire. The pupil took it into his head to avail himself of this opportunity. Taking up his big stick, he let it fall on the head of the master, who was then stooping over the cooking pan to stir its contents. But the pupil's stick was caught by the master with the cover of the pan. This opened the pupil's mind to the secrets of the art, which had hitherto been kept from him. He then, for the first time, really appreciated the unparalleled kindness of the master.[99]

These two passages, juxtaposed speak for themselves.

---

[99] Ibid, p 81-82

Conditions of a Solitary Bird

Now I will move to my final frame for comparison, existentialism. Here we find a modern refinement of ideas examined earlier. And, most importantly, this philosophy is similar to a philosophical strain, which runs through the entire Castaneda series, and this sets this position apart from all the rest.

The existentialists, as those others discussed in this chapter, seek to define reality in terms of individual perception. This, as we have shown, is at the core of all the teachings discussed, including those of Don Juan. But, while the existentialists try simply to define how the world is built around our perception and the eastern philosophers discuss methods for achieving the realization of the separate reality, Don Juan tries to instill a more definite view of what is and what is not. Perception is not totally individual because all sorcerers "see" certain things in the same manner. There is sub-cultural agreement by sorcerers about the nature of the sorcerer's separate reality just as there is cultural agreement about certain aspects of reality in a country like the United States.

The ideas that the world is incomprehensible could find a niche in all of these philosophies except in perhaps the philosophy of Plato. With the existentialists; however, this view transforms itself into the belief that the world is absurd rather than merely incomprehensible. But, with Don Juan, there is another twist. For, although things may be incomprehensible or absurd, Juan makes a very important distinction between worthless and unimportant. In a passage from a <u>Separate Reality</u> Don Juan proceeds from Carlos' lead to voice this distinction. Carlos is talking of an older friend who had died in a home for the aged, miserable, and feeling as if he had wasted his life.

The last time I saw him he had concluded our conversation with the following: "I have had time to turn around and examine my life. The issues of my time are today only a story: not even an interesting one. Perhaps I threw away years of my life chasing something that never existed. I've had the feeling lately that I believed something farcical. It wasn't

Conditions of a Solitary Bird

worth my while. I think I know that. However, I can't retrieve the forty years I've lost."[100]

Don Juan points out that when he says, "nothing really matters" he doesn't mean it the way Carlos' friend did. That man was "after victories and found only defeats…he'll never know that to be victorious or to be defeated are equal." The source of Carlos' conflict is that Juan had told him that every act he performed was "controlled folly" or that he acted as an actor would every single time he acted. However, his acts were sincere because he chose to be responsible for those acts and to act appropriately, or impeccably, for every occasion. To Don Juan everything is equal in that it is not any more important than any other thing. "I didn't say worthless," he points out. "I said unimportant."[101]

The end result then may be that our actions have no meaning because of a knowledge of an

---

[100] Castaneda, A Separate Reality, p 87

[101] Ibid, p 87

impersonal and unconcerned universe (as with the existential view) and the knowledge too of our impending deaths, but we can choose to act as if our actions were important. And we must therefore, with both the existential and sorcerer's perception of reality, take responsibility for our acts.

For the eastern philosophers, the struggle is to obtain the "truth" and to gain harmony with the world. Plato talks, in metaphorical terms, of mankind's climb from the darkness of the cave. For him too there is a possibility of enlightenment. The existentialists have their platonic counterpart in Camus' version of the myth of Sisyphus: of endless punishment to struggle pushing a large boulder up a hill only to see it fall again to the bottom. Camus sees positive existential possibilities with this myth.

His fate belongs to him. His rock is his thing. Likewise, the absurd man, when he contemplates his torment, silences all the idols . . . I leave Sisyphus at the foot of the mountain. One always finds one's burdens again. But Sisyphus teaches the

Conditions of a Solitary Bird

higher fidelity that negates the gods and raises rocks. He too concludes that all is well. This universe henceforth without a master seems to him neither sterile nor futile. Each atom of that stone, each mineral flake of that night-filled mountain, in itself forms a world. The struggle itself toward the heights is enough to fill a man's heart.[102]

The struggle is everything then. The symbolic struggles for enlightenment or from the cave have led us to Camus' sturdier symbol for existentialism, and existentialism leads to Don Juan and a new metaphor.

Our death is waiting and this very act we're performing now may well be our last battle on earth . . . I call it a battle because it is a struggle. Most people move from act to act without any struggle or thought. A hunter on the contrary, assesses every act; and since he has an intimate knowledge of his death, he proceeds judiciously, as if every act were his last battle. Only a fool would fail to notice the advantage a hunter has over his fellow men. A hunter gives his last battle its due respect. It's only

---

[102] R. Ellman and C. Feidelson, The Modern Tradition (New York: Oxford University Press, 1965), p 852

natural that his last act on earth should be the best of himself. It's pleasurable that way. It dulls the edge of his fright.[103]

---

[103] Castaneda, Journey to Ixtlan, p 85

6. ANTHROPOLOGY OR ART?

When we arrived, Black Elk was standing outside a shelter made of pine boughs. It was noon. When we left, after sunset, Flying Hawk said, "That was kind of funny, the way the old man seemed to know you were coming." My son remarked that he had the same impression; and when I had known the great old man for some years I was quite prepared to believe that he did know, for he certainly had supernatural powers.
--from Black Elk Speaks

"Don Juan! I didn't expect to find you here," I said. He laughed; my surprise seemed to delight him. He appeared to have been waiting for me.
--from Tales of Power, p. 11

I looked at Rolling Thunder. He had no mosquitoes on him. I stared hard at him. Swarms of mosquitoes hovered about him, darting back and forth, but none touched his face.
--from Rolling Thunder, p. 130

It was a warm day and the flies kept on pestering me A but they did not seem to bother don Juan. I wondered whether he was just ignoring them

but then I noticed they were not landing on his face at all.
 --from <u>Journey to Ixtlan</u>, p. 49

You cannot learn to be a medicine man like a white man going to medical school. An old holy man can teach you about herbs and the right ways to perform a ceremony, where everything must be in its proper place, where every move, every word has its own, special meaning. These things you can learn like spelling, like training a horse. But by themselves these things mean nothing. Without the vision and the power this learning will do no good. It would not make me a medicine man.
 from <u>Lame Deer Seeker of Visions</u>, p. 3

I was conditioned to believe that everything he did had some meaning.
 from <u>Teachings of Don Juan</u>, p. 72

It doesn't matter what one reveals or what one keeps to oneself .... Everything we do, everything we are, rests on our personal power .... If we don't have enough personal power, the most magnificent piece of wisdom can be revealed to us and that revelation won't make a damn bit of different.
 --from <u>Tales of Power</u>, pp. 16-17

Conditions of a Solitary Bird

The Indians did not have a written language so the older people had to be encyclopedias of knowledge that could be passed from one generation to another.
--from The <u>Memoirs of Chief Red Fox</u>, p. 19

Such things are very secret .... One member of a diablero's family has to learn what the diablero knows, Diablero's have their own laws, and one of them is that a diablero has to teach his secrets to one of his own kin.
--from <u>Teaching of Don Juan</u>, p. 5

I was riding into the woods along a creek, there was a kingbird sitting on a limb. This was not a dream, it happened. And I was going to shoot at the kingbird with the bow my Grandfather made, when the bird spoke and said, "The clouds all over are one sided."
f--rom <u>Black Elk Speaks</u>, p. 16

The sudden cry of a falcon woke me up .... The chase was over. It was going to be a difficult shot. I was lying on my back and the bird had its back turned to me. There was a sudden gust of wind . . .I suddenly felt a chill up my spine and in an unprecedented action I stood up and left. I did not even look to see if the bird had flown away.
--from <u>Journey to Ixtlan</u>, p. 32

For several hours after drinking the brew, I found myself, although awake, in a world literally beyond my wildest dreams. I met bird-headed people, as well as dragon-like creatures who explained that they were the true gods of the world. I enlisted the services of other spirit helpers in attempting to fly through the far reaches of the Galaxy.
--from "The Sound of Rushing Water," p. 28

The paste was cold .... When I had finished applying it I straightened up .... Don Juan was staring at me. I took a step toward him. My legs were rubbery and long, extremely long .... And from there I soared .... I pushed up with both feet, sprang backward and glided on my back. I saw the dark sky above me, and the clouds going by me .... I tried to look around, but all I sensed was that the night was serene, and yet it held so much power.
--*from* The Teachings of Don Juan, *pp. 127-8*

The quotations that begin this section are only a few of *hundreds* I uncovered, which graphically illustrate textual similarities between the Castaneda works and accepted non-fiction, ethnographic literature of the same genre to which Carlos claims his work belongs.

Conditions of a Solitary Bird

All of the selections are from books or articles that have characters (like Don Juan) that belong to the American Indian shamanistic tradition. All of these characters have been verified, by a number of sources as actual, living human beings. For example, Rolling Thunder, whose Anglo name is John Pope, is an active leader of the American, Indian Movement. Lame Deer and Red Fox both have their photographs appearing on the covers of their books.

At first glance it might appear that the only reason I might be presenting these excerpts is to align myself with critics such as Joyce Oates and Richard DeMille to prove that the Castaneda works are plagiarisms. However, if one examines the publication dates of the works quoted one finds that in most cases the events in the Castaneda works precede their counterparts in the compared works. I am not trying to indicate that Doug Boyd, Rolling Thunder, Chief Red Fox, Lame Deer, Richard Erdoes or Michael Harner plagiarized Carlos

Castaneda either. My point is directed at the very core of what I feel is the ultimate scientific question one should ask about the relative success or failure of the Castaneda works. *It is not a matter of fictitiousness or factuality, but of anthropology or art.* Are these works anthropology? Are they art? In the end the answers to both these questions I feel should be *yes*.

The case for the tetralogy being classified as art is probably the more popular and easily defendable. In the preceding sections I believe a great enough compilation of evidence has been presented to support this case. But do the books come up to the scientific standards that they must to be rightfully called anthropology? If this question can fairly be answered in the positive then too an answer will be made to those, such as Richard DeMille, who questioned the ethics of the board who awarded Carlos Castaneda his degree. "Why in short," DeMille asked smugly "has no scholar criticized what happened at U.C.L.A. or asked what the professors thought they were doing when they ratified Castaneda's fantasies?"[104]

In answering this question I went to the kind of person that DeMille admitted he was not, a scholar. When beginning this study I visited Professor Philip Newman who headed the committee that "ratified Castaneda's fantasies." This man was neither embarrassed, apologetic, confused or mystifying when answering questions about his old pupil? He was friendly and direct and told me in essence that there was no question in his mind that what Castaneda had done had earned him his Ph.D. The question to Professor Newman and his colleagues was not *Does Don Juan exist?* but rather, Do the books describe in a factual and enlightening manner the tradition that Carlos professed to be writing about? The importance did not lie in the description of Don Juan, an individual, but in the realistic presentation of Don Juan, a model, type or

---

[104] Richard DeMille, Castaneda's Journey: The Power and the Allegory (Santa Barbara: Capa Press, 1976) p 65

archetype for the medicine men, shamans, witches, singers, seers and brujos that do exist and whose methods of knowledge are outside the grasp of the usual enquirer.

"Ethnographic literature is of a very broad kind," Dr. Newman said. "Your own Mark Twain was a kind of ethnographer not in that he described actual events or people in Tom Sawyer or Huck Finn but because people reading those books know that the events and characters described are of a kind that could and did exist in the context in which they were presented."

Professor Newman ended our brief talk by giving me a list of books that might help me clarify this point in my own mind. Several of the books were anthologies or collections of stories that I would have before called only myths. In these stories birds and other animals talked, people changed their forms, and a series of (in our terms) impossible feats were performed. No one professed that these stories were factual accounts but here was the head of the anthropology department of a California university stating that these stories, like Castaneda's accounts, were anthropology.

Naturally not all anthropologists consider Castaneda's works as credible, let alone hold them in high regard. The professional sarcasms range from the inferred insult to the outright attack.

At the milder and more questionable end of the spectrum we find those such as Fernando Benitez who at the same time scoffed at Castaneda's achievement while riding on the coattail of his popularity. In a book entitled, straight-facedly, <u>In The Magic Land of Peyote</u> Benitez chronicles his own pilgrimage with the Huicholes on the sacred ritual of a peyote hunt. This book self-admittedly "should not be read as an anthropological work, but as the personal observations of a well-informed, humanistic, and erudite chronicler who brings to his craft substantial insights drawn from anthropology."[105]

Castaneda is mentioned in the introduction, but his name is sandwiched between a statement about "alienated middle class romantics" and an important distinction between writers such as Castaneda and anthropologists who "like to count themselves among those whose impact on traditional cultures is minimal and whose appearance on the indigenous scene results in the least amount of destruction and change."[106]

Clearly the implication is that this work (filled with numerous substantiating photographs) is somehow better or "more scientific" than some of its predecessors, including the works of Castaneda. The cover of the paperback edition clearly shows that this work is not entirely indebted to the "old

---

[105] Fernando Benitez, In The Magic Land of Peyote (New York: Warner Books, Inc., 1975) p 19

[106] Ibid, P 18

school," however, by announcing in bold print, above the title, "a revealing, first-hand report from the world of Castaneda's Don Juan." Enough said about Benitez.

At the other end of the spectrum is probably the most damaging Castaneda detractor, not only because the man is the most respected anthropologist in the field of aboriginal Americans and their use of hallucinogens, but also because he was once counted in the ranks of Castaneda's admirers. This man is Gordon W. Wasson. Supposedly Wasson "smelled a hoax" from the very first readings of the Teachings but was respectful for what he thought Castaneda was attempting to do . . . bring ethnobotany to the public.

Mr. Wasson was understandably dismayed at Castaneda's revelations about "smoking hallucinogenic mushrooms" with Don Juan since he (Wasson) was one of the very first western men to be allowed access to first-hand knowledge of shamanistic ingestion of these hallucinogens. He had heard of Indians swallowing and even drinking a concoction of these so-called magic mushrooms but never smoking them.

Other incongruities and unfortunate similarities between Castaneda's accounts and Wasson's are plentiful. Castaneda writes that Don Juan's mushrooms "turn to dust" on their own while Wasson reports that his dried mushrooms had retained their shape for more than six years and could not be crushed into dust.[107]

One of Wasson's main (verifiable) characters was named Don Juan and in his works a Mazatec named Genaro is mentioned. Wasson writes of a curandero[108] named Don Aurelio: "we had been talking with a curandero for days, all unawares."[109] Castaneda writes, "I had known Don Juan for a whole year before he took me into his

---

[107] DeMille, p 46

[108] Curandero, a term used to denote a curer of medicine man.

[109] DeMille, p 60

confidence."[110] Aurelio was blind in the right eye and Juan tells Carlos that a sorcerer's left eye usually has a strange appearance. The list goes on.

A final source of controversy and a barrier to academic acceptance comes with the translating from Spanish to English that Castaneda was supposed to have done. Not only does he fill Don Juan's mouth with numerous English idioms such as "the real McCoy," "cut the guff," "don't lose your marbles," and "golly" but tells us he is translating literally at some points where literal translations were impossible. The adjective "weird" for instance is Don Juan's favorite but has no suitable counterpart in the Spanish language.

What does all this mean? Does this prove, as Richard DeMille suggests that anthropologically Castaneda's works owe more than they contribute? I think not. What he fails to acknowledge is that there are justifiable answers to all the questions that he

---

[110] Carlos Castaneda, The Teachings of Don Juan: A Yaqui Way of Knowledge (New York: Ballantine Books, Inc., 1969) p 2

raises. "Juan" and "Matus" are names as common in Mexico as "John" and "Smith" are in the United States and "Genaro" is so common that Castaneda himself gives it to two entirely different characters in the same book. Wasson's mushrooms and Juan's are reportedly of different species and are contained, differently. (Wasson's are left in the open air while Juan's are kept sealed in a gourd for a year.) Wasson's mushrooms needed to be eaten to extend their properties but he admits knowledge of others using a drinking concoction and it is not impossible that the same mushrooms could be utilized in still another way (smoking). I personally have met several individuals who say that they smoke some kind of mushroom. Also there are more than mushrooms in Don Juan's smoking mixture.

As for the translation, one must take into account the cultural factor. When one translates they must not only be concerned with the "letter" but also with the "spirit" of what is being translated. Any student of cross-cultural literature knows that some phrases, especially idiomatic or slang phrases, from one culture simply would not make sense if translated "word for word" into any other language. A good translator must, therefore, substitute meanings at times for meaningfulness to realistically portray a culture's personality.

At best then Castaneda is a fine "emic" anthropologist with a flair for translating from Spanish into English not only the specifics of a sorcerer's teachings, but the complexity of a remarkable individual's and culture's personality, ideas and sense of humor. It's a remarkable feat. At worst Castaneda's feat is not anthropology in a traditional sense, but, like Benitez his observations are those of "a well-informed, humanistic and erudite chronicler who brings to his craft substantial insights that are drawn from anthropology," at least enough to earn him a Ph.D. in the subject without the aid of any sorcery.

Gordon Richiusa

Conditions of a Solitary Bird

7. CONCLUSION of Original Thesis

We come now to the final section of this study and as we do I am reminded of one of Don Juan's conversations with Carlos following Genaro's description of his journey to Ixtlan.

"What was the final outcome of that experience, Don Genaro?"' I asked.

"Final outcome?"

"I mean, when and how did you finally reach Ixtlan?" Both of them broke into laughter at once.

"So that's the final outcome for you," Don Juan remarked. "Let's put it this way then. There was no final outcome to Genaro's journey. There will never be any final outcome. Genaro is still on his way to Ixtlan."[111]

We have, in the preceding chapters discussed the Castaneda series from as many perspectives. We

---

[111] Carlos Castaneda, Journey to Ixtlan: The Lessons of Don Juan (New York: Simon and Schuster, 1972) p 264

have followed Don Juan's own dictum and seen that the true reality (the total critical perspective) lies where one can weasel between those myriad of views. One of the beauties of the Castaneda works stems from the "impeccability" from any and all perspectives. Looking just at the author alone these works are worth our study as literature from a biographical standpoint. As philosophical works they rank perhaps with those of Camus. They have brought a new dimension to the serial novel, perhaps even creating a new genre, the open-ended novel or novel without conclusion. There can never therefore be an end to our study. And as these books have come up to the above standards they have created one of the greatest characters and relationships for the reader since Don Quixote and his friendship with Sancho Panzo, supplying enough facts about the characters, enough successes and false starts to at least give the impression of true to life accounts.

Conditions of a Solitary Bird

Don Juan describes "impeccability" as the condition of acting appropriately in any and all situations or as Cyrano put it "to be in all things admirable." Castaneda's impeccability lies in his ability to express his ideas, on every level convincingly.

When he, using Don Juan as his ingenious mouthpiece, discusses something as simple as the relative attributes of the crow as the optimum bird, the argument becomes sheer poetry.

No other birds bother them except perhaps, larger, hungry, eagles, but crows fly in groups and can defend themselves. Men don't bother crows either, and that is an important point. Any man can distinguish a large eagle, especially an unusual eagle, or any other large, unusual bird, but who cares about a crow? A crow is safe. It is ideal in size and nature. It can go safely into any place without attracting attention.[112]

---

[112] Carlos Castaneda, The Teachings of Don Juan: A Yaqui Way of Knowledge (New York: Balantine Books, Inc., 1969) p 183

And we have already shown that the narrative mouth-piece could hold the reader spellbound when talking about the difference between "looking" and "seeing."

In our discussions, our viewing from several perspectives, we have seen that the Castaneda works are indeed fine literature from the individual as well as the cumulative view. And we have learned that although our discussions have been of a cursory nature they have been enlightening on this one important Don-Juanian point, and here I will quote one final time from the Castaneda works: "At this precise point a teacher would usually say to his disciple that they have arrived at a final crossroad . . . to say such a thing is misleading though. In my opinion there is no final crossroad, no final step to anything."[113]

To conclude then we can really arrive at no definite conclusion when discussing the Castaneda

---

[113] Ibid, p 227

Conditions of a Solitary Bird

works except to say that they are powerful and impeccable from each and every perspective. I for one will never again, after reading these works, be able to watch a crow flying without wondering if it is trying to tell me something. And never again will I be able to read or hear the words "look" or "see" without pausing to contemplate their distinction.

Gordon Richiusa

Conditions of a Solitary Bird

APPENDIX

The following pages are abstracted from Carlos Castaneda's dissertation; constituting the only difference between Journey to Ixtlan and the dissertation.

ABSTRACT OF THE DISSERTATION
Sorcery: A Description of the World
by
Carlos Castaneda

Doctor of Philosophy in Anthropology
University of California, Los Angeles, 1973
Professor Philip L. Newman, Chairman

This is an emic account of an apprenticeship of sorcery as it is practiced by the American Indians of modern Mexico. The exact cultural boundaries of the phenomena described here were never determined; and the conclusion I have arrived at, after years of fieldwork, is that sorcery does not have a cultural focus, but is, rather, a series of skills practiced, in one form or another, by all the American Indian societies of the New World.

The data that comprises the present work was gathered over a period of ten years of sporadic fieldwork in north-western Mexico, under the guidance and tutelage of a Yaqui Indian sorcerer, don Juan Matus, who in 1961 took me as his apprentice. Although I was not permitted to tape-record or photograph any event that took place during that time, I took notes and thus recorded in writing all the instances of our teacher-disciple relationship.

The main premises of this thesis, being an emic account, were statements voiced by the sorcerer-teacher. They pertain to the nature of the perception of reality. The sorcerer's contention is that the world at large, or our physical surroundings, which appear to have an unquestionably independent and transcendental objectivity, are the product of the perceivers' agreement on the nature of what they perceive. In other words, we, the perceivers, are the dynamic parts of the world, because we not only imbue it with meaning but also with "form." Thus the perceived realness of our surroundings is due to social consensus, rather than to its objective nature.

This basic premise of sorcery does not deny the objectivity of the world. For the sorcerer the world is not an illusion, quite the contrary, it is real, but its realness is not a fixed condition. In fact, it can be altered in part or it can be changed altogether; thus the alleged magical properties of sorcery practices. This possibility of change is called "stopping the world," and can be explained as the volitional interruption of ordinary consensus. The "techniques for stopping the world" entail that at the same time that ordinary consensus is interrupted another one is ensued and in this way a new "description" of the world is brought into being.

The present emic account, therefore, deals with the "techniques" by virtue of which a new agreement about the nature of reality is attained with its concomitant, a new perceptual reality.

In the present work then, the teaching of sorcery, has been taken as a process of resocialization and sorcery, in general, has been taken as a case of an alien "membership" made available to the non-member, in this case myself. The end result of this apprenticeship has been understood as the act of gaining membership. To have membership in sorcery therefore, means that the initiate becomes intimately familiar with all the known instances of the new perceptual reality he set out to attain.

—Carlos Castaneda, from Ph.D. Dissertation.

BIBLIOGRAPHY
For Gordon Richiusa Thesis

Books

Abrams, M. H. The Mirror and the Lamp. New York: Oxford University Press, 1953

Benitez, Fernando. In the Magic Land of Peyote. New York: Warner Books, Inc., 1975

Boyd, Doug. Rolling Thunder. New York: Dell Publishing Company, Inc., 1974

Castaneda, Carlos. The Teachings of Don Juan: A Yaqui Way of Knowledge. New York: Ballantine Books, Inc., 1969.

A Separate Reality: Further Conversations With Don Juan. New York: Simon and Schuster, 1971

Journey to Ixtlan: The Lessons of Don Juan. New York: Simon and Schuster, 1972

Tales of Power. New York: Simon and Schuster, 1974

DeMille, Richard. Castaneda's Journey: The Power and the Allegory. Santa Barbara: Capra Press, 1976.

Graves, Wallace and William G. Leary. From Word to Story. New York: Harcourt Brace Jovanovich, Inc., 1971

Herrigel, Eugen. Zen in the Art of Archery.: New York: Vintage Books, 1971.

Lame Deer, John Fire, and Richard Erdoes. Lame Deer Seeker of Visions. New York: Simon and Schuster, 1972

Myerhoff, Barbara. Peyote Hunt: The Sacred Journey of the Huichol Indians. New York: Cornell University Press, 1974

Neihardt, John G. Black Elk Speaks. Lincoln: University of Nebraska Press, 1961. (Reprinted from 1932 edition, William Morrow and Company.)

Noel, Daniel. Seeing Castaneda: Reactions to Don Juan, Writings of Carlos Castaneda. New York: Capricorn Books, 1976.

Red Fox, Chief. The Memoirs of Chief Red Fox. Greenwich, Connecticut: Fawcett Publications, Inc., 1971.

Wasson, Gordon R. Maria Sabrina and Her Mazatec Mushroom Velada. New York: Harcourt Brace, 1975.

Mushrooms, Russia and History, Volumes 1 and 2. New York: Pantheon Publishing Company, 1957.

Articles

Boyd, James. "The Teachings of Don Juan from a Buddhist Perspective." Christian Century, March 28, 1973, pp. 360-363.

Castaneda, Carlos. "Abstract of the Dissertation, Sorcery: A Description of the World." Dissertation Abstracts International, June, 1976, p. 5625b.

Cravens, Gwyneth. "Talking to Power and Spinning with the Ally." Harpers Magazine, February, 1973, pp. 91-94, 97.

"The Arc of Flight." Harpers Magazine, September, 1974, p. 43.

"Don Juan and the Sorcerer's Apprentice.'" Time, March 5, 1973, pp. 36-45.

First, Elsa. "Don Juan is to Carlos as Carlos is to Us." New York Times Book Review, October 27, 1974, pp. 35, 38, 40.

Furst, Peter. "Huichol Conceptions of the Soul." Folklore Americas, June, 1967, pp. 39- 106.

Harner, Michael J. "The Sound of Rushing Water." Natural History, June-July, 1968, pp. 28-33, 60-61.

Keen, Sam. "Sorcerer's Apprentice." Psychology Today, December, 1972, pp. 90-92, 95-96, 98.

Kennedy, William. "Fiction or Fact." New Republic, November 16, 1974, pp. 28-30.

Margolis, Joseph. "Don Juan as Philosopher." In Daniel Noel, Seeing Castaneda: Reactions to Don Juan, Writings or Carlos Castaneda: New York: Capricorn

Books, 1976 pp. 228-242.

Oates, Joyce Carol. "Anthropology or Fiction?" (Letter). New York Times Book Review, November 28, 1972, p. 41.

"Don Juan's Last Laugh." Psychology Today, September, 1974, pp. 10, 12, 130.

Gordon Richiusa

PART TWO
ReBoot

As predicted in my thesis written 1/2 century before now, the books kept coming even though the controversy raged over whether Don Juan existed at all. Things changed in the world and fabricating your own story (was called lying in the olden days) became common place.

In 2010, in ***The Five Principles of Everything*** I acknowledge the influence that Castaneda's writings has had on my work and me personally and solicited the help of 26 notable contributors as to how they interpreted the Five Principles. The more ways you can say the same thing the better (I've always believed), because we all hear (and ultimately learn and utilize information) differently (I say *selfishly*).

Until now, I have not published for the general consumer my thesis, though I have become an often published journalist with an understanding that people are often much more interesting that they may initially seem. Everybody really does have a story to tell.

I also developed a love of magical realism, often combining the two types of writing with some of my novels/plays/screenplays, 1) **Shidoshi: The Four Ways of the Corpse**, 2) **The Panda Chronicles**, 3) **Moon Dance**, 4) **The Wonderful World of Plagues,** 5) **Sticks Have Power, Shoes Don't**, and 6) **The Liquid Sphere** as well as hundreds of essays, new articles, scripts and true stories presented in the same way Castaneda presented his alleged anthropological works. Some examples include: **Pieces of Aloha**, **Heroes' Hearts Companion**, and **Ode To Life! The Love Story**.

Castaneda not only affected me in my own writing but how I taught everything from martial arts to English. the Legends and Legacies format for most of my books was based upon an understanding that how we learned and taught was predictably very intertwined with the stories we are told and how we hear them.

I have kept to similar format here, but as usual with my own particular twists. Without regard to the misguided (in my opinion) question of whether or not Carlos Castaneda's books are fiction or fact, I asked for help from a number of academics and other qualified and interested parties. Many of these individuals have contributed to other projects such as The ***Five Principles of Everything***.

Gordon Richiusa

Conditions of a Solitary Bird

Literary Lessons and Capsules

Before we conclude let's look more closely at the title of this book, related information, and other notes. For instance, I'm a dyslexic.

As a dyslexic-teacher I always focused my lessons to be clear to myself as well as any other student. I realized early on that I needed to use every type of memory device to remind myself of the importance of valuable lessons. I created my own symbolic language for taking notes which relied heavily on pictures (mostly arrows of varying sizes). I also created what I call Capsules, or single leafs of paper, sometimes both pictures and a few words, which I feel are the essence of a lesson. I created capsules for everything from archery to zoology including things like English grammar or writing techniques. In 1998 I was in a car accident that apparently triggered a flare-up of a disease called multiple sclerosis (commonly MS) which I did not know that I had until that moment. Suddenly, I could not think clearly or remember details. The doctors I was seeing thought I had traumatic brain injury from the accident or was experiencing problems because of years of martial arts. I was shocked!

All of a sudden I could not answer even the most simple of my students' questions. Luckily I had created a *capsule* for everything. Many of these now appear on a free education wiki/website I created called Vision-Revision. I literally had to relearn everything I taught, but with the advantage of having already examined my teaching strengths and weaknesses. The Capsules were invaluable to me, and I found them extremely useful to my students as I always encourage creative means of expression from us all. Using imagery to convey messages aides in communication as well. I favor bird images. The cover One such capsule related to

Conditions of a Solitary Bird

The San Juan De La Cruz poem, **Conditions of a Solitary Bird.**

Aside from the title and other details about the author I noted, "This poem details what it is like to strive for success, being one's own best example (martial artist, teacher, writer, etc.)." I added, "This is a good, graphic example of how to write a good paragraph, story, or poem."

Conditions of a Solitary Bird

The conditions of a solitary bird are five.
The first is that it flies to the highest point;
The second that it aims its beak to the skies;
The third, is that it does not suffer for want of company, not even of its own kind;
The fourth, that it has no definite color;
And, the fifth is that it sings very softly.
     —San Juan De La Cruz

Gordon Richiusa

8. A SECOND RING OF POWER

We are told in, *A Second Ring of Power*'s preface that this book was written about a year after the last book ended by an almost painfully unchanged Carlos Castaneda.

True to Castaneda's style, the contents are exactly what the title implies. *A Second Ring* begins with an acknowledgement of the leap into the abyss (the cliff hanger) that readers were left with in *Tales Of Power,* and remember, in *Tales* an enigmatic Don Juan concluded his teachings with apprentice Carlos by stating simply that when someone fails in their bid for power in the sorcerer's world, or worse yet never bids at all, then what Carlos has witnessed and reported becomes simply that, *Tales of Power*. Here we see that the story of sorcerers and apprentices can continue and will do so, with or without either Don Juan or his dumbbell apprentice.

Don Juan and Don Genaro are both gone, but Carlos sums up their affect on him as a kind of aphorism for the motivation a warrior's actions in life: "a most pressing need, the need to make headway in the midst of apparently insoluble contradictions."

In ***Second Ring*** we are introduced to or enlightened about the other apprentices of both Don Juan and Genaro, and especially a group of Sorcerer-Cohorts includes some very great women characters. As with other of Castaneda's creations a particular, fearsome initiate named Dona Soledad has been given the task by Don Juan and Genaro to become what Carlos apparently needed all along, *A Worthy Opponent*. This is a person who is on the same path of power that Carlos has been on and in the same way she is lacking. Her goal is to try and kill Carlos to take his power from him. Sh

In fact, women take front and center of most of the rest of the next books. In the preface we're told that all of the women were not only performing a

Conditions of a Solitary Bird

"final assault on his reason, designed by Don Juan himself," but in a few days help Carlos define the two "practical aspects of their sorcery;" The Art of Dreaming and the Arts of Stalking.

9. THE EAGLE'S GIFT

A continuation of **The Second Ring**. La Gorda is featured more prominently and we learn that Carlos is a little different from the rest of the Naguals, *energetically*. In this book we change from hearing Carlos frame his story from the point of view of a abject apprentice to accepting La Gorda as his *other half*. The Eagle is a warrior's representation of the immensity of the universe which Don Juan called The Spirit. The Gift of the Eagle (the Spirit) is that a true warrior can defeat death by slipping through the eye of the Eagle at the moment of death.

10. THE FIRE FROM WITHIN

The fire from within is how sorcerers and impeccable warriors perceive how they will be consumed at death...by a fire from within. This view of death corresponds to one of the versions of how humans end their lives. Since energy can neither be created or destroyed, consumed by one's own energy and absorbed into eternity is a realistic way of projected how our bodies might be destroyed. Another alternative is to allow ones energy to be absorbed by the Earth, which is also becoming popular these days whereas people are opting for a burial without a crypt at the base of a tree for example.

Don Juan and Don Genaro (the first ring of power we assume) are reintroduced into the writings because we learn of various levels of "attention" and a sorcerer's trick of teaching their apprentices in the second and even third attentions.

11. THE POWER OF SILENCE

Readers were so happy to have Don Juan back in the books that this one is subtitled: In these Further Lessons of Don Juan the reader gets a first hand look at a sorcerer's training that takes place on more than one level. We get practical experience with Doing as opposed to Not Doing, and some of the other details we learned about in the first four books. We also learn the fine differences between a benefactor and a teacher, as one works primarily with the first and second and the other with the third attention. In this regard Don Juan's benefactor, Don Vicente is introduced, as is the Nagual Don Elias.

12. THE ART OF DREAMING

Beginning with an explanation of *The Sorcerers of Antiquity*, this book turns out to be one of my personal favorites.

Dreaming (not just having a dream, but setting it up and maintaining it) is one of the greatest feats of a sorcerer. Carlos, as one of the two naguals (replacing Don Juan and Don Genaro) has learned to DREAM in this manner and also to SEE (become aware of conglomerations of energy directly).

We learn that there are various layers of awareness (like skins of an onion, we're told) and of something called an *assemblage point*, which is typical of all human. We are human because our awareness is focused on a particular spot in our energetic being. This energy blob also varies and looks different for those who are average humans, warriors, sorcerers, and even naguals. Where our assemblage point is in the blob makes us the kind of person we are. Our behaviors and ways we think and feel about things also have influence on where we assemble our awareness in the egg. The practices of the sorcerer, warrior, and others helps us gain control over where our assemblage point remains. Usually it is kind of stuck in one general

Conditions of a Solitary Bird

place, but there are ways to knock it loose and see the world from a totally different place. Learning the art of dreaming is one of those techniques.

Dreaming in the second attention.

Dreaming positions so that one can learn to dream while already dreaming, to achieve a heightened level of control.

Meeting and exchanging energy with the DEATH DEFIER.

Learning that while dreaming in this way that the people who are in your dream and are NOT creating energy (because they are part of your dream) may have their own thoughts.

The name Carol Tiggs is introduced and seemingly the somewhat fragile veil is lifted between Carlos's apprentices in the verifiable world and the stories he has been telling.

13. MAGICAL PASSES

Like Tai Chi, Yoga, Martial Arts or other mind/body/spirt practices and other ritualistic actions, Magical Passes are a series of movements which help a Warrior-Practitioner store and access power or energy. I covered these practices at the Los Angeles Convention Center for Campus Magazine where I caught a glimpse of Carlos himself, roaming the halls of the center, riding up and down the escalators. He was dressed in a stylish, grey, three piece suit and paid no attention to anyone. The women (and some men who were their associates) were conducting a class with hundreds of would be *warriors* in one of the large meeting rooms. The practices are alleged to have been given to the blue scout (probably Patricia Partin aka Nuri Alexander) by ancient sorcerers, death defiers, and spiritual allies as this one person was said to have gained the power to move between the universal realms. The techniques played on the belief that we all have an energy field around us that can be manipulated through repetitive movements. At one point, the Scout was shuffled swiftly out a hidden doorway in the wall. I guessed that they were trying to disappear in sorcerer fashion, so I bolted out the door and ran down a stairway to the parking lot. My instincts paid off when the group came out of an elevator and I was already standing nearby. The scout (unlike Carlos earlier on the escalator) stopped and acknowledged me with a glance before climbing into a waiting car.

14. THE WHEEL OF TIME

This is one of my most referred to books and is a favorite of those who are not interested in slogging through the entirety of the Castaneda series. This book is a collection of quotes from all the previous books making Carlos and the rest accessible to all rather than just those who have been totally immersed in the sorcerer's journey.

15. THE ACTIVE SIDE OF INFINITY

This book cannot be simply placed as the final book in the Castaneda series. *Active Side of Infinity* is a singular achievement much different than all the rest. It is really outside the scope of comparison. It is, of itself A Solitary Bird. Although this 15th book in the series is attributed to Carlos Castaneda's authorship, it was published the year AFTER Carlos died!

There is much speculation as to what this means, but I think there is a likelihood that the last several books were co-authored by the group of women who had taken over Castaneda's writings in the publication of *The Second Ring Of Power*. In fact, several of the books which followed the first (and some that do not appear in this list) were entirely written by others, especially women or men who claim to have been taught by other cohorts of Don Juan (e.g. Don Miguel Ruiz in his series starting with The Four Agreements, and Sorcerer's

Conditions of a Solitary Bird

Apprentice: My Life With Carlos Castaneda by Amy Wallace).

Gordon Richiusa

16. RECONCILIATION & DSS

When I hear people ask, "How can they believe that?" The royal "they" usually means some group or individual to which you've arbitrarily assigned opposing views. This is the Dragon-Slayer syndrome at its most blatant. Remember, I am saying these things completely devoid of the self-delusion of any religious beliefs of my own, yet with plenty of first hand-experience in organized religion.

I recently read yet another brilliant Substack article written by the great Kareem-Abdul Jabbar. One short paragraph caught my attention fully, because it succinctly stated the Dragon Slayer Syndrome's biggest flaw: *"Mobs are lazy thinkers, willing to unburden themselves from the responsibility for forming their own opinions by adopting others' pre-fab opinions, then hide their shame by shouting those stolen opinions loudly and bullying those who don't agree."*

Let me explain how coming to terms with this psychological human trait can be seen as both the cause to all our problems, as well as the answer to them, *or both of these at the same time. Every Human is a Solitary Bird.*

Allowing yourself to be your own best example, may seem impossible under the conditions I'm talking about here, but it is at the core of what I'm declaring as ESSENTIAL for individuals to live life comfortably or to come together as a society. It is a PROCESS I call: RECONCILIATION. Remember, this is what I've distilled as a martial arts based Five Principled way of dealing with solving problems . In Five Birds Self Defense we believe that Defense Awareness as it is better to solve problems before they occur rather than simply reacting to dangers at the last second.

Conditions of a Solitary Bird

As a life-long martial artist, a dyslexic who became a successful journalist and teacher of English Literature, archery, swimming, tracking and stalking among other "special skills" I decided to gather together 26 various contributors from a wide spectrum to do one thing: simplify a Life Strategy which is based on human traits and tendencies and not dogma. I decided to do what my teachers had done for me...Teach by example...knowing that the most important person anyone can ever teach is *oneself.*

We all have different tendencies, skills, strengths and weaknesses. We don't need to agree on what those strengths, tendencies, weaknesses, or skills are. If you don't believe that there are shared human qualities or that honest reflection is required for each individual to smoothly blend with all the other individuals in the world, then you should stop reading this right now. If you can accept that this idea, then let's move forward.

So, in 2012 I composed and compiled and sent a copy of a book entitled, **The Five Principles Of Everything** to every member of Congress (every Congressperson and every Senator), every U.S. Governors' office, and every member-nation of the United Nations, as well as many presidents, corporate leaders, scientists, religious leaders, teachers, students and others. **The Five Principles of Everything** has been translated into Spanish, Italian, with proposed translations in other languages. Although, I admit a bias for English, partly because it is the language of the Internet, and partly because of my dyslexia. I am anemic to the concept of learning other languages.

Here, let's pretend for a moment that actual dragons do exit, or maybe let's simply agree that they might have existed are a memory of something that we expectedly experienced in the past...in some form at some point. There are certainly enough examples in printed literature, films, television, and even oral tradition to convince us that dragons must have lived at some point in history. Debating that question is not important to the understanding or acceptance of the syndrome we are talking about here.

For our purposes I've done a casual survey and almost arbitrarily come up with these qualities:

Characteristics of being a dragon:

1) Innately Possess great Magic/Power, Wisdom, and Wealth

2) Has Ancient Knowledge and Spiritual Strength.

3) Can become ferocious if attacked or those they love are attacked.

4) In tune with both the seen and the unseen forces of the Earth and Nature.

Characteristics of being a Slayer:

1) Admires (to the point of Coveting) Magic, Power, Wealth

2) Sees History and Religion as tools to manipulate in the pursuit of #1

3) Knows that it is impossible to *become* a dragon, so instead simply attacks what it admires.

4) Notoriety ordained by some other authority, often represented as Divine Authority.

I presented this idea to a married couple who I knew to be good, ethical, and moral people. Not only did each of them easily pick a side, but they assigned a side to their partner as well. The problem? Even after I gave them my sketchy characteristics, they could not agree on any part of the subject. While one thought their spouse was a dragon, the spouse thought they were a slayer

Conditions of a Solitary Bird

ONLY because they thought of dragons as dangerous and that they were going to have to protect their spouse from the danger!

When I was in my late teens I liked to hitchhike up and down the western United States, often the California to Oregon coastline. One day I was standing in the San Fernando Valley, on the Topanga Canyon onramp that led to the 101 freeway north. My destination was the Big Sur area where I had created a small encampment with a inside a giant redwood tree. I had learned somewhere that I had a better chance of getting a ride if I had a sign that told drivers where I was heading. My BIG SUR sign was not really cutting it for me, so I borrowed a pen from a nearby vendor and scribbled on the reverse of the paper I'd been holding the words, "BE A LIBERAL." Almost immediately when the first group of cars came by, a woman slammed on her brakes and backed up to me. "I AM a liberal!" she shouted, opening her door. Imagine having such a sign today, and what the results might be, especially if the hitchhiker was a woman or a person of color?

Just 10 years previous to the hitchhiking event, I was in elementary school in the principle's office for having made a girl I thought was pretty cry. I called her a *communist*, not knowing what the word actually meant, other than it got a rise out of her. When I was called into the teacher's room and reprimanded, I literally asked for a lunchtime trial to defend my right to say what like. The wise teacher told me that the "trial" would be the next day and I remember quoting from the Constitution and rambling on for a minute before the teacher put a halt to the next day's proceedings. "No new evidence," he stated simply and added, "Please just try and not call names."

As a follower of many false paths, I have come to understand that it is never enough to believe something...You want others to believe it too. On the opposite side of this fence is the fear that others are constantly trying to make you feel hopeless

Conditions of a Solitary Bird

because focusing on out there keeps us insulated from what's going on inside. So, offering contrary views becomes the only real hope. This is another aspect of this syndrome at work. It's important to point out however, that I am not being a conspiracy crank just because I try to stop a bunch of other groups and individuals who believe differently that me, are benefiting...from the same things that I am. The reason there are cliches is not only because a majority of people believe something, but because a certain path has proven to be workable at some level for a large number. Maybe a characteristic of those belonging to that group is a belief in the duality of our existence. Perhaps we are all both Dragon and Slayer and not necessarily does that mean that we are at our best or worst at either or both ends of this spectrum. Intermitant and random reinforcement is more powerful than no reinforcement at all. It's why people will pull a slot machine's handle all day long, even though they never hit a jackpot!

I'm always impressed by the elegant and varied solutions humans can find to solve the same problems. We are in the end uncontrollable problem solvers inflicted with DSS.

My best advice in this regard is: **_Neither feed the dragon, or try to slay it._** If there were dragons they can take care of themselves. They don't need your groveling support, and trying to slay one as a empty exercise at best. Yet, any step in the right direction is a step in the right direction no matter how small and ill conceived.

So what are we left with? There are no such things as Perfect Dragons or Dragon Slayers.

In the martial arts there are a large number of individuals (many calling themselves Masters, Grandmasters, and other elitist titles) who pretend that their (fill in the blanks as you wish) teacher, method, weapons, style, technique, understanding is somehow better than all the other ways. In truth, there are only so many ways one can move their hands and feet (if someone is inclined and able move their hands and feet at all.

In the course of my chosen professions, I've had occasion to defend myself against multiple or sometimes much bigger opponents; I've been attacked by old and young fanatics holding knives, guns, boards, chairs, chains, broken bottles, or other weapons. In the Five Principles of Everything I describe how I defeated over 30 opponents with nothing more than words. The point is, I prevailed in each case, but I never thought that those times were really a test of my martial skills even thought they clearly were. Why do we diminish our successes if they don't meet some arbitrary standard?

Because I had trained myself to continually test and modify my skills in even the smallest actions, deeds, or thoughts I thought the only true test of my skills was whether I physically defeated my attacker. That simply is erroneous. Again, in the

Five Principles I point out that the only self-defense technique or strategy that works every single time is avoiding conflict!

Right away there are those reading here who will say, "But what about bad guys? What about when we're attacked? Are we supposed to simply let ourselves be injured or worse?" To my mind, if you are attacked you simply haven't avoided conflict. That's a whole different thing, and not what I'm talking about here.

Luckily I've had good teachers, and good examples. I've applied my martial skills to the *slings and arrows of outrageous fortune* on a daily basis, creating little games, checks and modifications at every turn PRIOR to being attacked. These are the important lessons that I use to help me teach others whatever it was that they thought I was teaching them. In the end, I believe this perspective helped me be a better teacher overall, because I was teaching about *learning* solely by example. I prevailed, I survived, I am endlessly optimistic and

Conditions of a Solitary Bird

I have not only recovered from attacks, but deadly diseases, injuries, anger, loss of loved ones, the unknown because in essence I practice an attitude and a mindset...not techniques.

Imagine what will be humanity's fate two or one-hundred thousand years from now. What do you want it to be? Is your personal best inevitable? Is your personal best even pertinent? Are these questions even worthwhile to the individual pursuit of happiness? What role does your happiness play in achieving what's inevitable? Is there both collective consciousness and collective responsibility? To my mind, these questions are not worthy of my pursuit. I am human and forced to make choices and take actions on an ever changing playing field with ever changing rules and boundaries a I myself am changing.

In this environment I CHOOSE my beliefs. I choose to believe that I get to choose the path(s) I follow--if only to the degree that I when I die I will be content in the thought that I lived my life *as if* I had free will.

The level of belief in anything (how you think and feel about things, affects your chance to benefit from it) changes the power of it. In other words, anything can be powerful (magical if you like) but to varying degrees, affected by the level of belief. the more you believe, therefore the more powerful. Psychosynchrosimpiosis. A wafer and a sip of wine are meaningless without the belief that these are representations of the body and blood of Christ.

Weapon Stupidity is an example I use to explain how mistaking a Strategy for a Tactic will likely lead to failure. With this example I describe to martial and self-defense professionals how training with weapons or even a single style can lead to problems when the weapon or style being used (perhaps by your opponent against you) gets knocked to the floor or otherwise becomes useless. The inferior martial artist might dive for a weapon that is dropped, perhaps even fighting over it

Conditions of a Solitary Bird

without noticing that the person who actually wanted to do you harm no longer has the use of this tool. The weapon is not likely to be a threat on its own. In other words, one cannot fight the weapon. They are fighting the opponent. Tactics are attention to the weapons. Strategies deal with defeating opponents, but moreover strategies help us deal with living a better more efficient life. On the larger scale, more than knowing who your enemies are we should probably should focus on who is trying to hurt you, who is hating you and *why*.

What if everything we've ever thought or heard about dragons and dragon slayers has been a supplanted idea? Humans are suckers for their ability to use words. We even write things down TRYING to make them true. We name things in the way we want them to be, not necessarily how they really are. It is how the Pacific Ocean got its name. In the study of linguistics we call this naming ***nomenomen***.

All the good (aside from actually being true, because we've already suspended that measure of reality in this essay) we know comes from either being a THIS or a THAT may have been created under very false-pretenses. All the bad we know about something is spawned in the same sewer as the good…the belief that the only strategy that works is this one you chose is ludicrous. That's really the crux of every argument, spat, quarrel, disagreement.

In many martial arts there is an idea called Triangulation. Triangulation is seeing every action (offensive or otherwise) *indirectly*. If you are a point on a triangle (or any belief or position you hold) and someone you oppose is another point, what is the third, or shared perspective on this same triangle?

In the case of every current problem in the world we're constantly being asked to choose, "Are you a Dragon or a Dragon Slayer?" Are we required to pick one side over the other till the literal end of human time? I do not think so. There is always at least a third option, which is devoid of ego and selfishness allows each of us to simply not engage, to avoid conflict. In The Five Principles we say that there are always five ways to measure every thought and deed. No one principle is the ONLY principle. When we start thinking too narrowly, I call that being "Weapon Stupid" because we cannot just look at the weapon as being harmful. The person holding any weapon always has other weapons (including the best one, the brain) at their disposal.

When it comes to politics, family, war, crime & punishment, daily decisions we need to learn the power of triangulation. Who do I choose in a terrorist attack? I do not choose the terrorist. Terrorism is bad. I oppose it. Who do I choose in a war? War is bad. I oppose it. Discrimination of any sort is bad. I oppose discrimination and abuse in all forms. Win without war to me means that one does NOT need to kill people to be a hero. Bruce Lee famously said that he had learned, "the art of fighting without fighting."

Encouraging discrimination, terrorism, war, abuse of power are all examples of weapon stupidity on the part of individuals. Reconciliation is not simply giving up to bullying. It is an individual act of balancing self preservation with our collective consciousness.

As if there is always a MUTUAL BENEFIT…it has the feel of truth, because even a bold faced lie is based on the belief that there *is* a truth that needs to be concealed.

Today, due to worldwide communication, excessive numbers of people, and a growing knowledge that our individual actions, thoughts and beliefs may cause worldwide calamities, disease, and/or destruction we are are learning that we are all in the process of recovery from something. Humans are also full of optimism. We believe there is an effective treatment for every ill, resolution to every conflict.

The reason that disinformation uses stolen valor and other logic tricks is because while (for instance) one party is calling the other traitors, spenders, polluters, liars, cheaters, and perhaps worse is because it's irrefutable that these things exist. What the "stolen" part points out is that they are themselves the things they're accusing the other of being. Dragons defend themselves by becoming Slayers and visa-versa. Like me in elementary school. Like you in (fill in the blank). Our lives are finite. We might as well live our lives with an understanding that Point A (our births) and Point Z (our deaths) are the things that bring us all together. We all only really have an iota of control over the parts in between, but literally each little decision can rightfully be called a life and death decision. In the end, even if this control is only an illusion, we are still going to have to make endless choices on our individual paths. How we teach ourselves to make all our choices is probably the most important decision of them all.

The character Don Juan made his disciple recount every memory, every detail of his life that brought him to the place where he would accept the construction of reality that was presented as sorcery. I believe this process to be completely personal and essential to our individual happiness. It is simply to me a process of coordinating our individual and collective consciousness and is the foundation for all decision making and problem solving. I call it, The P*rocess of Reconciliation* and believe it should perhaps be taught in all schools, at home, and everywhere. Why? Because change is inevitable, problems arise and we must choose a path. Recovery, Rehabilitation, Redemption, and Reconciliation are really all the same in that they are processes (established or discovered paths) with the same goal…helping us to individually navigate our individual hopes and dreams with our natural collective natural human tendencies.

Anyway, that's what I think. I have decided it is time to put these ideas in writing because I am a writer. I'm acting *AS IF* my efforts have meaning.

The first one hundred pages of this book are nearly verbatim my Master of Arts thesis, written over 50 years ago (from the time of the publication of this edition). That analysis of Carlos Castaneda's first four books (**The Teachings of Don Juan: A Yaqui Way of Knowledge, A Separate Reality, Journey to Ixtlan,** and **Tales of Power**) was submitted as partial fulfillment of my Master of Arts degree requirements in English Literature, at the California State University in Northridge. The work has sat until now, in the archives of the Oviatt Library--checked out by a few enlightened souls who still physically appreciate libraries--because it is only with the test of time that I've determined that the Total Critical Process that I employed to analyze Castaneda's works originally, has proven the most important premises of the work, simply because this has become a gold standard for all honest investigation.

Here is two foundational assumptions of the original thesis:

1) Carlos Castaneda would have an incredible impact on the many fields of academic and spiritual investigation and 2) his books should rightfully be considered as literature within their own specialized genre as an open-ended, serialized, journalistic novel.

In my thesis I coined the term **Psychosyncrosymbiosis** for the specialized relationship that a "character and narrator" in a book can have with the "real person" who is doing the writing. In other words, the *Character Carlos* and the *Writer Carlos* needed one another, and each actually depended upon the other for their very existence. Today, I realize that this is the process that we all use to reinvent ourselves, sometimes daily. It is the essence of quantum physics where reality is energy expressed through vibrations. Our thoughts are affected by our environment and our environment is similarly affected by our thoughts.

I knew (at the time of the writing of my thesis) that more books would be written and, as it turns out, the process that I used in the first four books only serves to strengthen my original conclusions. Those other books will be analyzed in the second half of this text, in part, as I never gave the subsequent books the same close analysis that I did the first four. Now, I feel there is more reason.

However, I recommend that if you must choose between something like my book and any one of the books that Carlos Castaneda authored then you should choose Carlos. To me it always seems preferable to make up ones own mind. However, if you become interested in hearing what others think about the Castaneda collection, I would like THIS to be the best place to start. Why? This is the only total critical analysis. We will not take sides in what are ultimately unanswerable arguments.

Now that the human being Carlos Castaneda has passed from this Earth, we can get on with the business of examining his legacy as well as focusing on any single, narrow aspect of it. I believe his import and impact in a Total Critical sense is indisputable. Even at the writing of my thesis I knew that more books were on the horizon. I hypothesized that, because the works were not presented as merely fiction the production of them *must* continue at least as long as Carlos Castaneda lived. He had written himself into a self-feeding pickle.

At the time I did not consider the obvious human conditions of mortality or the desire to "leave one's legacy" in my analysis. *Psychosyncrosymbiosis* (defined in the thesis as a condition where a writer is so closely associated with his characters that he falls prey to needing them to make sense of his own actual existence), in a sense is as much a curse as a blessing because we often create characters that are unrealistic and even archetypal for being both models for behavior and fatally flawed. This turned out to be a major sticky point that could have been rectified with time. Unfortunately, since others had been drawn into the story, as both characters and writers themselves readers and conspiracy theorists with little or no knowledge of original intent have also been absorbed into Castaneda's infinite loop. These days I am calling this problem: *The Dragon Slayer Syndrome*.

For, as time went on for Carlos (writer and creation) the responsibility of training apprentices (actual, verifiable human beings and those who only believed they knew the books) forced Castaneda to seek apprentices to write about themselves and their work with Carlos (the Nagual) in the same way that Castaneda the author wrote about Don Juan. Some took it upon themselves (as people often do) to have an opinion founded entirely on hearsay and speculation, drowning out honest academic inquiry.

Amy Wallace, (the daughter of Irving Wallace, with whom she co-wrote **The Book Of Lists** and earned credibility as a serious writer) and I spoke several times prior to her death. She produced a marvelous book (in 2013) that claimed to be a memoir of her close association with Carlos Castaneda, calling herself one of his *wives*. It chronicled a turbulent and weird relationship, in which, she said, she learned that Carlos was more of a trickster than a selfless guru. For the most part, I believe it was an accurate account of her life with Carlos and the other *witches*. We were communicating because I had sent her a copy of **The Five Principles of Everything** (in which I mention Castaneda and my own thesis).

In her book she claimed to have been treated bizarrely by Castaneda, as well as the other apprentices, and eventually she broke away from an association with him and his inner circle.

Conditions of a Solitary Bird

According to her, Carlos never told her that he had made up the whole Don Juan story, but that her suspicion--based solely on her own observations--was that he'd, at least, greatly exaggerated the claims made in his books. In addition, Amy claimed that *martial arts practice* was a requirement by Carlos, for anyone who wanted access in the inner circle of daily human life.

She also claimed that Carlos had less and less input into the writing of the subsequent books after **Tales of Power,** which was the final book he wrote when I published my thesis. Also, she was not really sure that he was the primary writer of the fourth book in the series, because the style got "more and more literary." These suspicions were unfounded by fact, and she acknowledged that much with me, conceding that Carlos may have simply *gotten better as a writer* as he went along.

As you can see—and as I realized 50 plus years ago when my attention was caught by a fascination for Casteneda's work—once

Psychosyncrosymbiosis gets rolling, it seems to create its own momentum and appears to have an ever increasing thirst that needs quenching or both living beings (the dreamer and the dreamed) cease to exist; even though a half century has passed, I too find myself caught up once again in the process. That's why I have decided to re-publish my thesis to be used as a point of reference for any and all examinations of the visible works and legacy of Carlos Castaneda, but from an evolved perspective.

Naturally, as an English teacher and lover of words with my own definition of *literature* we start by assuming that these books are, in fact "literature," regardless of whether they are non-fiction or mere fantasy.

For that reason here I have emphasized one very important premise: The works of Carlos Castaneda are some of the most important literary works EVER written. Some might find that statement too bold, but notice that I emphasize "literary works."

Conditions of a Solitary Bird

In my thesis I merely touch upon the importance of literature to our daily lives. Here let me state emphatically, *"All true literature has one important thing in common. It teaches us about life and how to live it."*

A final measure of a literary works' lasting value comes in how many basic human themes and individual lives are affected. Carlos Castaneda is one of the most quoted (and plagiarized) authors of all time. Even those satellite works (including Tensegrity workshops and books written by those most closely associated with his legacy i.e. The Three Witches and others beginning with Castaneda's own Second Ring of Power") continue to illuminate new directions in the search for meaning in our lives. There is no denying the success of such things as, **The Secret**, or **The Four Agreements** for instance, or even my own **The Five Principles of Everything**.

I often have assigned readings from the first four books to my own students in various disciplines, as examples of inspiring technique and juxtipose these readings with other great literature and imagery (i.e. I Know Why the Caged Bird Sings by Maya Angelou and Emily Dickenson's There is No Frigate Like a Book).

The truth is, if it wasn't for Carlos Castaneda, no one would use the term "spiritual warrior" as we do today, and we might not have been introduced to a 15th century Franciscan monk and poet from Mexico named San Juan de la Cruz, in one of the most artfully crafted short poems entitled, **_The Conditions of a Solitary Bird_**.

Carlos Castaneda was indeed one-of-a-kind but he also acknowledged his debt to others. Most of us do not realize what we owe to Carlos Castaneda, especially for his contributions to a whole new kind of magical realism that transcended the boundaries between fact and fiction, both positive and negative. I personally appreciate his accomplishment beyond measure, even if he was completely mad or a charlatan of an order only equaled by the likes of those who create whole worlds and mythologies out of thin air. Indeed there are easy comparisons to many modern day individuals whose lives blur the lines between fact and fiction, truth and lie.

In this edition of **The Conditions of a Solitary Bird**, I add two important measurements for the importance of the Castaneda series. First, as I did in **The Five Principles of Everything**, Using Carlos-Juan as a model, I tell true personal stories about magical moments in my life, moments that perhaps I would never have given a second thought to if it weren't for my involvement with both Carlos Castaneda and martial arts.

As both a teacher of martial arts, and a college professor or curriculum writer of many subjects I have learned the value of storytelling. Some think that I'm good at it. That makes me happy. Another of the things I've learned from the Castaneda books is that every person can do the thing that makes them happy and call it an act of power.

Gordon Richiusa

Carlos Castaneda was indeed one-of-a-kind. Most of us do not realize the debt we owe to Carlos Castaneda, especially for his contributions to a whole new kind of magical realism that transcended the boundaries between fact and fiction. I appreciate his accomplishment beyond measure, even if he was completely mad or a charlatan of an order only equaled by the likes of those who create whole worlds and mythologies out of thin air. I also now see the dangers of confusing the lines that are sometimes painstakenly created by those who simply do not understand the power of words

One story we touch upon within this text is about a man named Od Nordlund…a cultural anthropologist who (in the 1940's) was considered an expert in Symbolic Language. He was a guy who saw that shamans from many cultures were somehow taping into an "over-voice" (my term) that seemed to communicate with a logical "voice" through various means that tapped into core human intuitions. In one story, after explaining that a *seer*

Conditions of a Solitary Bird

in a certain village had been asked to "find the herds of game" which the people relied upon. The seer went into a trance (perhaps using hallucinogenic drugs, perhaps not) and through some effort spoke with his spirit helpers about the location of the herd. When he came out of the trance, he could accurately predict exactly where the herd would be found. The hunters went to the location (sometimes many miles from where they were) and found the game. Skeptics would argue, "he's not really talking to any spirit guides. He has been brainwashed by his teachers, through storytelling mixed with orally transferred facts, to know that when the geese flew through these parts, 20 years ago, with the same numbers of members in the flock and they stayed for the same amount of time, and the muskrats fur was the same length, and the rains had fallen in the same amounts, and the snow lasted to the same time, and the grasses were in the same abundance etcetera, that the herds were in the same place that he was predicting. The seers brains were like computers communicating through symbolic logic

Od looked at these people and said simply, "What difference does it make? It's still incredible!"

Finally, I introduce you to a person who I've come to admire above all others for her wisdom, skill, and example, far more than any idealized version of a Person Of Knowledge that you may have read about in some other books. Her name is Michelle Manu, someone who epitomizes all the best qualities envisioned by those who followed Carlos on his version of The Warrior's Path, until they were disillusioned by his shortcomings. Michelle is, in my opinion *A Solitary Bird* of the most admirable kind…and she's not influenced by CARLOS CASTANEDA!

She's been introduced to some of my and others favorite passages, of course, even the poem by San Juan de la Cruz, which inspired the title of my thesis and this book, and she's heard from others who know his work and even call themselves

Conditions of a Solitary Bird

sorcerers. In her book, ***The Archetype of The Woman Warrior*** she discusses bird symbolism of a similar bird to one we find on the cover of this book. However, what I usually tell her about passages from Carlos' writings is to only let them influence her thinking in response to one of her own observations, thoughts, or comments!

Knowing that there are people like her who respond directly to the morality of the warrior's way, as I wrote about in ***The Five Principles of Everythin****g*—not because of manipulation by a third party (the master, teacher, celebrity or benefactor said so), but through intuition (and in that way perhaps directly to human concept of The Spirit though a heightened appreciation for life) has given me a renewed sense of hope for the future. Through nothing more than the open, unadulterated exchange of ideas through conversation, I hope to arrive at this agreement:

No matter how flawed the Warrior Way of Castaneda might be, or futile trying to become a

Gordon Richiusa

Sorcerer, Celebrity, Master, General, Priest, or Person of Knowledge, there still seems to be an advantage in our daily dealings to choosing a personal path where magic reigns over pessimism or nihilism. In addition, most of us feel the same way about the word **science** *as we do about the word magic. .*

A person of knowledge might only know that every system is flawed, but chooses to follow the **Path With A Heart** because any true warrior's path would always err on the side of magic, wonder, truth, beauty, and love.

Humans are basically optimistic so, as a teacher, I could not help but share Kumu Manu's wisdom with you, and you won't have to go searching in the deserts of Mexico or the Southwest U.S.A. for the privilege. To those who continue to be blinded by DSS and the question of whether Don Juan was a real person or not, I will answer with the words of Od Nordlund, "What difference does it make?"

Conditions of a Solitary Bird

A wonderful short poem by a dead, white, male poet (Robert Frost) cuts right to the heart of this point:

FIRE AND ICE
by
Robert Frost

**Some say the world
will end in Fire,
Some say in Ice.
From what I've tasted of desire,
I'll hold with those who favor Fire.
But if It had to perish twice,
I think that for destruction Ice
Is also great, and would suffice.**

Gordon Richiusa

17. LIVING THE WARRIOR'S LIFE

by

Michelle Manu

I am Michelle Manu. I am many things (including a legal professional with a Juris Doctorate) and am known as a Senior Black Belt and teacher (Kumu) of the rarely seen ancient and modernized Hawaiian Warrior Martial Art, the Lua, Kaihewalu family lineage. I began my martial arts training at age nine, reluctantly and have ended as the only woman to reach my level of proficiency and be given the title and responsibility of Kumu under Grand Master ('Ōlohe) Solomon Kaihewalu since the early 1980's. It is historic that I've achieved such accomplishments being of mixed descent, raised on mainland U.S., and a woman. To date, I am also noted to be the only woman in historic record to make Hawaiian weaponry. For almost 10 years, I toured the Midwest as a professional Polynesian Hula dancer and choreographer. I now use the Hula dance to demonstrate how Lua and Hula movements are one in the same. When the missionaries decided to bring native people into the light of Christianity, Lua, and many other cultural practices, were banned. When the fighting arts were banned in or around 1823, the Lua was concealed within the Hula. To date, we don't see the Hula and Lua communities mix as they once did in ancient times. Hawaiian Lua has always been considered and is still considered kapu (sacred) by those who are dedicated students, practitioners, teachers, and lineage holders.

Today I use the Hula specifically for my haumāna (students) to learn superior footwork, timing, balance, transition and micromovements of the feet, and how to efficiently manage and use the upper body with the lower body at the same time. This raises eyebrows, sometimes with disdain and other times with curiosity. To me, it – the Lua within the Hula and the Hula within the Lua - is open and obvious for those who have the fluency of both movement languages.

For some, Lua is just a martial art. Like Hula, Lua perpetuates that which was, that which is, and that which will be. While we wholly honor our foremothers and forefathers, we too, like they did, must evolve to today's world and the very real challenges of today's world.

Lua is not just a martial art. It was the cultural practice of the warriors throughout the generations. It was, and is, our sacred way of life. The warriors didn't just wake up, exit the hale (house), and do techniques all day. They were well-rounded and trained in war strategy, hula dance, astronomy, conditioning, Lualomi (warrior massage), navigation, architecture, medicine, fishing and more. This is how Lua is different from other martial arts. We are the equivalent of what the Spartans were to Greece and the Samurai was to the Japanese. We emulate nature elements and animal movements. Our first and only religion was the *metaphysical* (the unseen) and the *physical* (the seen). All was connected.

Today in the martial world there is sport martial, competitive martial, traditional martial, self-defense, and military or tactical martial. In my opinion, Lua falls under the last three categories. While it is traditional, it is also for self-defense and is combative. Think of our warriors on wa'a (canoes) and moving down the chaotic battlefield.

Conditions of a Solitary Bird

I love being a woman. I am free; free to express the soft or intuition and hard or intellect within me. There is no hard without the soft. The soft is the feminine or Hina, while the hard is the masculine or Kū. It is the wind up to the pitch in baseball, the knee bend of a hockey player for a push off, the arms bent for the release of the basketball, and the path to the contact of a punch.

In ancient Hawaii, there was no differential between these energies. All was and is one energy on a spectrum of expression. Today however, it is helpful for us to learn vocabulary for visualization and to help us understand what expression of energy we wish to become. This classification of duality provides for deeper understanding. We think that external martial arts is only Kū, but clearly it is not. These energies also play out in our world and how we communicate with one another.

Is there right and wrong?

I spent much of my youth believing all things were either truthful or not, right or wrong, awesome or stupid, and black or white. After much personal confusion, failure, things not going as they should, and believing what I was told, "You do this and 'Ta-Da!'... this will happen." I now believe there is no such thing as 'right' or 'wrong'. There is much gray in our existence. Just like there is the visible and the invisible and the physical and the non-physical. What may be 'right' for one spirit is 'wrong' for another. There is only what is beneficial and life-giving, or its opposite, unbeneficial and life-depleting. Any type of determination is exclusively subjective, and our choice is made on a moment-to-moment basis based upon our level of consciousness.

Conditions of a Solitary Bird

How do we know which is which? We think we know everything, or at least a lot. We also have nervous system programming in play at all times. All our knowledge is arbitrary at best as our awareness is always expanding. We are still discovering 'new' deep sea creatures and 'new' planets, stars, and solar systems. We rely on science and our awareness of discovering new things about our world is ever evolving.

There is a difference between 'knowing about' and 'knowing'. Then, beyond 'knowing' is to simply 'be'. Labeling such as 'right' and 'wrong' could be helpfully rephrased as either beneficial (right) which is life-giving for all involved, or unbeneficial (wrong) which is destructive or life depleting. To be beneficial, the choice must be fair to the decision maker (self-integrous) too, and not just for everyone else that is involved (enabling). As a result new answers, options, and experiences appear as choices ('free will'). As an example, who or what we were attracted to five years ago may no longer be attractive to us if we have evolved in our awareness.

What are the most admirable qualities of a warrior? It truly takes a lifetime of diligent conscious choices—sometimes very difficult and courageous ones—to live a warrior's way of life. When I think of my heritage of Polynesian, Asian, and Scandinavian in physical form, I think of a chiseled, finely tuned Polynesian, Viking and Asian male fighter with expert weaponry and hand-to-hand combat skills and mutant superhero powers; a version of the invincible boogie man. We relate the word 'warrior' to the physical. However, when we really take a moment to examine what it means to be a warrior, we realize that physicality is just one facet of our energetic warrior being. There are wounded and elderly warriors among us that no longer have qualities that the Western world would deem warrior-like. Contrary to what society would classify as old, ugly, beat-up and useless, I believe this makes them no less of a warrior but just in a different aspect.

We hear "warrior spirit" all the time. What does that really mean? When I think of the spirit of a warrior, I believe it means to possess skills beyond physical ability. During the lifetime of a warrior, I believe that he or she will possess, or work towards possessing, the abilities to communicate and comprehend; be steadfast and constant; be connected; develop and use discernment; accept and be non-attached; know thyself; devoted; know that everything is energy; and let go.

Communication and Comprehension

As warriors, we must learn to compassionately communicate with all types of people. To truly comprehend we must listen and attempt to understand from another's point of view in non-judging and loving manner, even when you know that the person's perspective is not beneficial to him or herself, or anyone involved. A warrior would then say, "Have you thought about this?" "Or, what if...?" The delivery and using finely honed 'soft skills' - tone and body language - are so important. Part of my professional life (also known as my alter ego) has been spent as a mediator. I have seen content get lost in delivery (context), which is usually accelerated at the speed of light when one party chooses to allow the animal brain to erupt in emotion. At this point all content is lost in context. It is very difficult to attempt to get the parties to regroup and restart after an eruption of the primal animal response. One party cannot control himself and the other is in fight mode because he is being attacked. Lame but this is how we are made and remain if we do not evolve to a higher level of consciousness. The ultimate goal of life, warrior or not, is self-mastery. This would include remaining in control of self at all times... ALL TIMES. This requires us to honor the pause when we are baited or triggered.

Steadfast and Constancy

Respect, honor, truth, allegiance, and so forth, are rooted in being steadfast and constant. Fits and starts of enthusiasm of new projects, jobs, and relationships should also be steadfast and constant. To properly allocate our mana (energy and power). This is what people expect of us if this is our historic mode of operation. However, is this beneficial? Does it produce respect (whether personal or professional), honor, truth and allegiance? I wouldn't want to be known as being steadfast and constant in erupting on everyone for anything at any time! As a warrior leader, I want to be known and respected for having control over myself and my responses (or lack of response). It doesn't end here. I am also known for being steadfast and constant in addressing less than respectful acts and behaviors by others. This has been a learned ability.

Connectedness

"Everything in the universe constantly lives off an identifiable energy pattern of a specific frequency that remains for all time. Every word, deed, and intention create a permanent record; every thought is known and recorded forever. There are no secrets; nothing is hidden, nor can it be. Everyone lives in a public domain. Our spirits stand naked in time for all to see.

Everyone's life, finally, is accountable to the universe." - David R. Hawkins, MD, PhD

"Every act or decision we make that supports life, supports all life, including our own. The ripples we create return to us." - David R. Hawkins, MD, PhD

Discernment

There is a lot of smoke and mirrored illusions of what we think we see and know. Discerning an issue and coming to the truth of the 'seen' and 'unseen' facts surrounding a situation may be difficult, but it is possible. In a calm spirit without prejudging a situation, we must courageously communicate with the involved parties instead of assuming they did or didn't do something, or feel or not feel a certain way. The more impartial we stay during this process, the freer the universe is to reveal all to us. To remove our fixed points of view.

I tell my students it is like a deck of cards. We can lay them out on a table, and they are just cards. It isn't until someone tells you what card game is going to be played that certain cards then have certain value. We will see what we seek to find. Impartiality and neutrality are best in every situation. Understanding may never fully come in some instances. We all have past events that resurface, and we still don't have the full understanding. For instances in progress, it is beneficial to support the solution without attacking the supposed cause or person. We can find completion in place of closure.

I believe that all truth is subjective and there is no such thing as objective truth. Even if objective truth existed, we would rely on our subjectivity to experience and understand this objective truth. As warriors, we need to respect others' right to their subjectivity.

Conditions of a Solitary Bird

Acceptance and Non-Attachment

We cannot fully understand all events we experience or witness. Acceptance is not apathy. Acceptance is the display of non-positionality that can then progress into non-attachment. Non-attachment is not detachment. It is simply being in a state of benign gratitude for the experience, however crappy it may be at the time – knowing that there is a lesson in this experience. Specification of context of the perceiver is just as important as the objective content. It is wise to give up the pursuit of trying to assign blame to others. Learning to accept, forgive, let go, and be non-attached brings an increased peaceful existence that promotes honesty, reduced defensiveness, and self-esteem. We come closer to achieving this by using both our intellect and intuition.

Know Thyself

All things start from, return to, and all answers are found within oneself. Nothing 'new' is really being learned. What we find during our growth is that, if we are connected with our Source (God) that the information was always there and waiting to be revealed to us. It will reveal itself when we are ready and in a state of mind and spirit to receive it. I don't know how many times I've said, "I knew that! Hmm..." 'Mistakes' and 'errors' are inevitable; however, I believe there are no such thing as mistakes and errors. For whatever reason why we made a choice, it was for our self-evolution; to learn from it. That is why people and events present themselves, to be assistive in our evolution.

It all starts from within – in then out – the body first as it tethers us to the physical, then mind, then spirit.

"Stand in your power and be confident in what you know. Never apologize for what you know." –Michelle Manu

Devotion

Intention sets devotion. Devotion to any person or endeavor is fueled by intention. Devotion is to show up, even if we don't feel like it and have a thousand fantastic excuses. Things happen and (re)align when we are in movement, freely exercising our creative choice. Showing up is the first step in devoting ourselves to a purpose or endeavor. Devotion is doing what we must (beneficial) regardless of how difficult it may be, even for a prolonged period of time. Warriors don't whine when fulfilling this purpose. They decide, show up, shut up, and complete their mission.

Everything is Energy

We are beings that emanate an energetic field into consciousness while being consciousness itself. There is no separation.

"A word uttered takes flight." – Hawaiian Proverb

All things are energy, including a thought. All things begin in the unmanifest and are born into the manifest – physical existence. When one chooses to make beneficial decisions, honors all living things through decisions, by and through intent and devotion, the individual's level of consciousness elevates - and because we are all connected - the overall universal level of consciousness elevates. As Friedrich Nietzsche said, we cannot remove one grain of sand without affecting the whole.

Let Go

An effective warrior benefits from having a clean body, mind and spirit. We must let go of the memories of events and people that are not beneficial when we still have an emotional response when the memory comes up. Letting go of past pains, events, and people allows us to be available to unlimited abundance waiting for each of us. With past pains still ripping at the spirit, we also invite energetic hitchhikers (entity attachments) that do not have our best interests at heart.

Fear, worry, and deep anxiety are to the metaphysician what the devil is to the usual church goer. This is true for me when I am heavy. It is a form of Hell on Earth for me. The devil is nothing more or less than the human mind to believe a lie and nurture it. This belief gives authority to the subconscious to continue the problem and intensify it. This misdirection of consciousness is what true blasphemy is.

When we stop authorizing negatives by our deep belief in them, they will occur less in your experience. The only evil power is our human mind when it is convinced that we are limited by the conditions of our experience. The saints are those who searched themselves and baptized their own thinking until it is crystal-clear, and they can be confounded no more. Leave good alone is true and Love alone is the answer.

The spiritual recognition of our subconscious as a divine instrument that produces our ideas of freedom and our loving the right use of them gives us the equivalent of Heaven on Earth. We know your Source and hold fast to intellectual thinking and intuitive feeling.

We cannot withdraw from life. The way of the hermit, religious recluse or fanatic is as much out of balance as the materially dominated individual. We will still have to meet ourselves, for we are always our own problem. Where you are, there is the Power of Life – through choice, authenticity, and adaptability.

Gordon Richiusa

Conditions of a Solitary Bird

www.ingramcontent.com/pod-product-compliance
Lightning Source LLC
Chambersburg PA
CBHW071905290426
44110CB00013B/1280